D0086369

Metamorphosis:

A Guide to the World Wide Web

&

Electronic Commerce

Metamorphosis:

A Guide to the World Wide Web

&

Electronic Commerce

Patrick G. McKeown and Richard T. Watson
Department of Management
The University of Georgia

John Wiley & Sons, Inc.
New York • Chichester • Brisbane • Toronto • Singapore

Acquisitions Editor	Beth Lang Golub
Assistant Marketing Manager	Leslie Hines
Senior Production Manager	Linda Muriello
Senior Designer	Karin Kincheloe
Cover Designer	Carolyn Joseph
Assistant Manufacturing Manager	Mark Cirillo
Cover Photo	Comstock

This book was set in 10/12 Palatino by Richard Watson and printed and bound by Hamilton Printing. The cover was printed by New England Book Components, Inc.

Recognizing the importance of preserving what has been written, it is a policy of John Wiley & Sons, Inc. to have books of enduring value published in the United States printed on acid-free paper, and we exert our best efforts to that end.

Copyright © 1996, by John Wiley & Sons, Inc.

All rights reserved. Published simultaneously in Canada.

Reproduction or translation of any part of this work beyond that permitted by Sections 107 and 108 of the 1976 United States Copyright Act without the permission of the copyright owner is unlawful. Requests for permission or further information should be addressed to the Permission Department, John Wiley & Sons, Inc.

ISBN: 0-471-13689-1

Printed in the United States of America

10 9 8 7 6 5 4 3 2

To our children
Ashley and Chris
Alice, Ned, and Sophie

Preface

In describing *Metamorphosis: A Guide to the World Wide Web & Electronic Commerce*, the most important aspect we want to emphasize is that this is "not just another Web book!" Instead, it should be viewed from two perspectives. First, it provides a thorough overview of the Web and the Netscape Navigator browser including background on client/server networks, the Internet, browsers, accessing the Web, creating Web pages using HTML, and accessing Internet resources using the Web. Second, it demonstrates the impact that the Internet and the Web are having on businesses and organizations. It is this second aspect of the text that clearly sets it apart from many other guides to the Internet, the Web, and Netscape. In addition, a disk with four complete Web sites accompanies the book thereby providing local Web access. Finally, there are many exercises throughout each chapter as well as end-of-chapter review questions and exercises.

Electronic commerce is clearly a rising tide in the world of business, and this book provides important information on how readers can take advantage of this trend to further their opportunities. The importance of being able to react positively to changes in technology is first discussed in Chapter 1 and then revisited in Chapter 6 where a unique approach to electronic commerce is discussed. Built around the concepts of the *customer service life cycle* and *integrated Internet marketing*, this approach provides the reader with a veritable "how to" manual on using the Web and Internet to further the aims of their organization. Without a doubt, Chapter 6 should be considered "required" reading for anyone interested in the coming world of electronic commerce.

In addition to the discussions on electronic commerce in Chapters 1 and 6, almost 70 companies and organizations are used to demonstrate electronic commerce in action. In most cases, each organization's Web site URL is also provided. These same URLs are available by linking to the Web site for this book.[1] By visiting these many commercial and organizational Web sites, the reader can gain great insight into the many ways the Web is being used.

---

1. http://www.negia.net/~webbook

Another unique aspect of this text is that the reader does not need to have access to the Internet and Web in order to learn about electronic commerce. This is made possible by the four Web sites that have been stored on a floppy disk that accompanies the book. This disk can be duplicated and distributed or the four sites can be transferred to a local hard disk or file server where they can be accessed. These four sites include Intellimedia Sports, Inc., Alberto's Nightclub, Rhebokskloof Estate Winery, and Jimmy Buffet's Margaritaville Store. In each case, the on-disk Web site includes many of the graphics found on the original Internet Web site. By accessing them in a local mode using the file:/// protocol, the reader can learn how the Web has been used commercially without taking up precious bandwidth. In fact, the book is set up so that the first four chapters can be covered without needing to access any remote Web sites. Only Chapter 5 on Internet resources and Chapter 6 on electronic commerce require that the user have access to remote Web sites. We believe that this feature will be especially important for those locales having limited or very slow Internet access or where many individuals might attempt to access the Web at the same time. This feature will enable the reader to experience and learn about the Web without depending on access to the Internet.

Another element of this text that will be of great use in the learning process is the *Your turn!* exercises, which are placed strategically throughout each chapter to reinforce the learning process by asking the reader to implement some material just discussed in the text. In Chapters 2 and 3, the *Your turn!* exercises make heavy use of the four local Web sites mentioned earlier. In Chapter 4, the student is asked to practice writing HTML statements. Finally, in Chapters 5 and 6, these exercises request that the student demonstrate an understanding of Internet resources and electronic commerce. In addition to the *Your turn!* exercises, there are review questions and exercises at the end of each chapter. Finally, there are key terms at the end of each chapter which are defined in a Glossary at the end of the book.

Acknowledgments

We would like to thank Tom Hall of Pitt Community College, Anthony Nowakowski of Buffalo State College, and Jennifer Thomas of CUNY, Baruch College for their outstanding reviews of the text. They made numerous useful suggestions. We would also like to thank Jason Airlie of The University of Georgia for his close reading of the manuscript. Lorena Akioka did an outstanding job of editing the text under less than favorable conditions. At John Wiley & Company, we would like to thank our editor, Beth Golub. We would also like to thank Carolyn McKeown for her reading of parts of the original manuscript and Clare Watson for proofreading the entire text. We acknowledge the contribution of The University of Georgia electronic commerce research group: Sigmund Akselsen (visiting from Telenor, Norway), Issam L. Almutawaly, Traci Carte, Mutlu Celikok, Monica Garfield, Barbara Haley, and Erich Lehmair. Finally, we would like to thank our family and friends for their support during the writing and desktop publishing process.

Patrick G. McKeown
Richard T. Watson

Table of Contents

1 Introduction to the Internet and World Wide Web

Objectives

After reading this chapter, you will be able to:

❖ understand the concept of creative destruction and the resulting revolution in business;

❖ discuss the importance of computers and networks to business;

❖ describe the Internet and its operations;

❖ discuss the World Wide Web and its impact on the Internet;

❖ describe the client/server relationship;

❖ understand the use of hypertext and multimedia on the Web;

❖ describe the use of Web pages and browser software;

❖ understand the importance of codification and distribution as they relate to information systems.

Introduction

Twenty-five hundred years ago, the Greek historian Heraclitus (c. 540-480 B.C.) said that "Nothing endures but change" and that statement has never been more true than today. Over the last forty years, information technology has relentlessly redefined the conduct of business. Old business practices are constantly being destroyed and new ones created. The accountant's leather-bound ledgers and journals have been replaced by computerized databases, and the typed letter has been replaced by electronic mail. Companies that have not adapted to these changes have gone out of business or been purchased by their competitors. For example, Smith-Corona, the last domestic typewriter manufacturer, filed for bankruptcy in July 1995 due to its inability to compete with the new generation of PC-based word processors and laser printers.

1

Successful organizations in this time of rapid change will make the required transformation by creatively destroying old ways of interacting with customers, suppliers, employees, and shareholders and then creating new ways. Like butterflies, who change from ugly caterpillars into beautiful creatures, organizations must make a metamorphosis. Becoming a butterfly is a radical change for a caterpillar, and business must recognize that to exploit the opportunities created by information technology, it may have to undergo a similarly amazing metamorphosis—a radical redesign of current business practices.

Creative destruction

Termed *creative destruction* by Harvard economist Peter Schumpeter, this concept emphasizes that the most important part of the change process for a business is not what *remains* after the change but what has been *destroyed*. Without a destruction of the old ways of carrying out business, we cannot create the new. Creative destruction often requires an entirely new way of thinking about the problems facing a business. Executives may need to redefine the problems or reframe the questions; simply doing business as usual will not suffice. For example, Reuben Mattus decided that he needed to creatively destroy his existing Bronx ice cream product in order to be successful. Rather than changing the ingredients or the formula, however, he changed the product name to Haagen-Dazs and raised the price. It did not matter that the name had no meaning in any language or that the same product now cost more, he had successfully redefined his approach to business.

The World Wide Web

A recently introduced information technology, the **World Wide Web** (or simply the **Web)** has begun to have a dramatic effect on business and organizations globally. It threatens to bring about large-scale destruction of existing business customs and the creation of new ways of doing business. The Web is the prototype for the "information superhighway" that has been so widely discussed in the popular media. If you are to participate in this business revolution, you must become familiar with the Web. That is the purpose of this book: to make you familiar with the Web and to learn how the Web will change the ways in which commerce is carried out. When you finish this book, you should:

know how to access computers that are linked to the Web;
understand the process of creating your own Web applications;
become familiar with the complete range of Internet operations;
understand the fundamentals of electronic commerce.

Information demand

One thing that has not changed in business and industry with the advent of information technology is the demand for information. Executives need information to help them make high quality decisions that will affect the overall success of their company or organization. These can be major decisions that will change the long-term strategy of the company or they can be day-to-day decisions that will affect the company in a less profound way. For example, senior IBM executives needed many different types of information to help them make the decision to purchase Lotus. At a different level in IBM, employees need information to decide which software product will help them do their jobs better. In either case, the person needs information to make this decision. In fact, information is fast becoming a very important asset for all types of organizations: corporations, governments, and not-for-profit organizations. Without a ready source of information, many companies could not continue to operate for more than a few days.

A new aspect of our dependence on information is the requirement of *speed.* In the not so distant past, we would have been happy to obtain information in a matter of days, weeks, or months. For example, as recently as World War II, the commander of the American forces in the Battle of Midway did not follow up his decisive victory because of lack of information on the extent of enemy losses. Civilians did not even know there had been a battle for several weeks. Today, with worldwide television coverage, it is possible to be informed of an event anywhere on the globe almost instantly. This becomes especially crucial in business and industry where a global economy requires access to the most up-to-date information in order to remain competitive. Whether it is a dramatic drop in the Dow-Jones Industrial Average on the New York Stock Exchange, a fire in a computer memory plant in Asia, or a new oil find in the Arctic, business people must have access to this information quickly in order to make the decisions that will determine how successful their companies will be in responding to the new development.

Acquiring information has historically involved searching through many publications. This search can be quite time-consuming, often involving a trip to the closest library. If you do not know the appropriate source, then you need to use various paper-based research aids to find the book or journal that contains the desired information. If the library does not have the desired material, then you will need to obtain it via an interlibrary loan. Today, the search for information is being made more efficient through the widespread use of **computers**. With a computer, you can enter a keyword and find sources of information that match the keyword. In some cases, the actual source information may be stored on computers making it possible for you to search for and retrieve the information electronically. There are now well over 175 million computers of all sizes in use around the world that, together, have the capability to store a virtually unlimited amount of information.

Nonetheless, the real key to universal information access is the capability of those computers to share information. Instead of stand-alone computers that would be useful only to those people who have access to a particular computer, we now have **computer networks.** In a computer network, computers are linked to one another over various communication media that range from telephone lines to satellite links over which they can exchange information.

Not only do computer networks enable us to carry out operations that would not otherwise be possible, they make it possible for us to search for and retrieve needed information very quickly. In fact, modern computers can find and retrieve a document or software file from a distant computer in a matter of seconds.

Types of computer networks

Computer networks can be classified as either centralized or decentralized. A **centralized computer network** is one in which there is one computer or a group of computers to which all other computers must be linked. Examples of centralized networks include the commercial computer networks like Prodigy, America Online, and CompuServe. These commercial networks now serve over 6 million people who use personal computers to call into central computers to carry out a wide range of activities. For example, a user of one of these commercial networks can exchange information with other users on electronic bulletin boards or through "chat lines," read news reports, track the stock market, and make airline and hotel reservations. Figure 1-1 shows a typical centralized computer network.

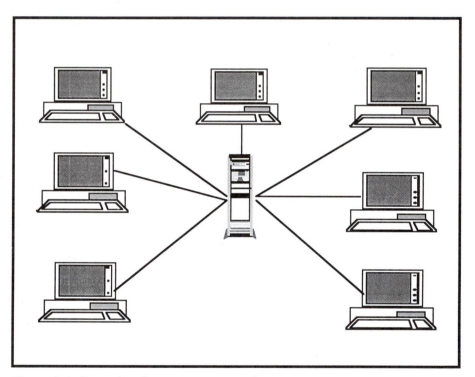

Figure 1-1. Centralized computer network

A **decentralized computer network** is one in which there is no one computer or group of computers to which every other computer is linked. Instead, computers are linked to other computers which are linked to still other computers and so on. A decentralized network can also be composed of smaller networks. Information is passed from one computer to another by passing through intervening computers. Figure 1-2 shows a decentralized computer network.

The best example of a decentralized computer network is the **Internet,** which currently has over 20 million users worldwide and is growing at a rapid rate each year. Virtually all universities in the United States now provide their faculty and students access to the Internet. Long used by professors

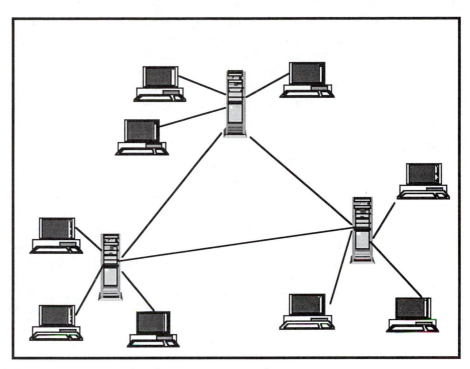

Figure 1-2. Decentralized computer network

and researchers to exchange or search for information, the Internet is now popular among many other computer users. In this chapter, we will introduce you to the Internet and its newest element—the Web.

The Internet: a network of networks

With millions of users worldwide, the Internet is the largest decentralized computer network in the world. Actually a *network of networks,* it is a linkage of smaller networks each of which agrees to use the same system of rules (called a **protocol**) for exchanging information. In addition, users on any network can exchange information with each other without having to know the physical location of the other user. The Internet protocol is called **TCP/IP**, which stands for Transmission Control Protocol/Internet Protocol.

A wealth of information is available on the Internet, including documents from individuals and organizations, e-mail lists, free software, access to other computers, drawings and photos, music and voice recordings, and video clips. While some of this type of information is also available on the centralized commercial networks, the sheer volume of available information is much greater on the Internet. For example, on the Internet you can:

❖ send and receive messages electronically;

❖ view information on the White House staff and the First Family;

❖ retrieve legislation being considered at both the state and national level;

❖ find free software, including games and utility software

❖ find photos of Richard Watson's ear operation.

Another dramatic difference between the Internet and the commercial networks is that many Internet users pay no individual fees to use it. In most cases, the costs of using the Internet are borne by the user's organization. On the other hand, a growing number of users access the Internet through the commercial networks or through companies that specialize in providing Internet access for a fee.

Internet history

The Internet began in 1964 as the brainchild of a Rand Corporation researcher named Paul Baran who was seeking a method to ensure that the Pentagon could communicate with members of the U.S. armed forces in case of nuclear attack. It was assumed that links connecting any two cities would be completely unreliable, so he suggested a totally decentralized computer communications network with no central computer and no overall governing authority. In a such a network, even if one or more computers is destroyed, it is still possible to send information between those remaining.

By the early 1970s, university faculty and other researchers found that, in addition to being a method of communicating with the U.S. armed forces, the Internet was an inexpensive way for them to communicate with each other. The Internet was made even more useful when the National Science Foundation (NSF) created a high-speed, long distance telecommunications network in the mid-1980s into which other networks could be linked. Although the NSF no longer supports this high-speed network, it is now supported by other organizations. The Internet made the news in 1988 when a Cornell graduate student unwittingly released a rogue program over it that caused some 6,000 Internet-connected computers to fail.

Until 1991, because the government subsidized the Internet, it was restricted to nonprofit, educational, and government organizations. In that year, NSF loosened those policies and allowed many new commercial sites, thus fostering the Internet's explosive growth. As a result, the commercial use of the Internet is an area of great interest to the many companies looking for business opportunities.

Internet operations

As mentioned previously, the Internet is a great place to acquire information through contact with other users or by finding information from a variety of sources. You can also acquire software or work on other computers. This can be done through a variety of **Internet operations,** shown in Table 1-1.

To carry out an Internet operation, the user provides an address of a computer somewhere on the Internet to a piece of software on a local computer, which then contacts the distant computer to execute the requested operation. For example, if you wanted information about a particular piece of legislation being considered by the U.S. Congress, you would enter the address of the computer that stores that information and the name of the document and in a matter of seconds, the document would be transferred to your computer

Table 1-1: Internet operations

Internet Operation	Purpose
FTP (File Transfer Protocol)	Retrieve files from a computer elsewhere on the Internet
E-mail (Electronic Mail)	Exchange electronic messages with other Internet users
Telnet	Work on a computer elsewhere on the Internet
USENET Newsgroups	Participate in a wide variety of online discussion groups
Gopher	Retrieve documents from a computer on the Internet using a menu-driven system
World Wide Web	Allow the transfer of text, images, sound to a local computer

Accessing the Internet

To use the many applications that are available on the Internet, you must first have access to it. This usually involves using a high-speed telephone line to connect to a regional network that in turn links into the **backbone** of the network. The backbone of any network is the primary high-speed communications link between major computer centers to which other networks are connected.

At one time, most organizations were linked to the Internet via their large mainframe computers. Today, however, the linkage to the Internet primarily involves personal computers (PCs) tied into the organization's local area network (LAN) rather than using a mainframe. The organization pays a fee to access the Internet but at this time does not pay a per user fee or a fee for usage time.

Individuals who do not have organizational access to the Internet may either access it through a commercial network like America OnLine and CompuServe or through a new type of company called an **Internet provider.** Internet providers are companies who specialize in linking organizations and individuals to the Internet as well as providing services to them. In the first case, the subscriber usually pays an hourly fee for access time while in the second case, they often pay a flat fee to access the Internet through the Internet provider. In either case, access to the Internet is through a PC and a **modem,** which allows the subscriber to call into the network via a telephone line.

A good analogy to the Internet is the interstate highway system in the United States (which coincidentally, was also set up in the 1950s and 1960s to create a way of moving the U.S. armed forces around the country). To use the interstate system (which is equivalent to the national backbone of the Internet), you first have to traverse your local community highway system, then possibly your state highway system, and then finally get on an interstate highway. With both the Internet and the interstate highway system, you move from a local network to a regional network and then to a national or international network. Figure 1-3 shows a typical connection of an individual PC to the Internet.

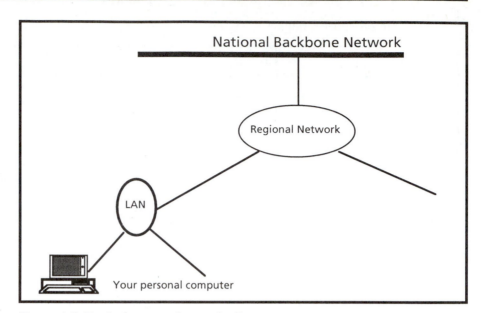

Figure 1-3. Typical connection to the Internet

Regardless of whether you are an organizational user of the Internet or an individual subscriber who is using a commercial network or Internet provider, you do not need to be worried about the technical details of using the Internet. It is set up in such a way that if you know the address of the person or computer you wish to contact, the software on your local computer and on the computer you are accessing will take care of the rest.

The World Wide Web

The newest addition to the Internet is the Web. Of all the changes to the Internet since its inception, the Web has brought the most radical changes and interest. Originally developed to allow scientists to easily exchange information, the Web is now the fastest growing part of the Internet as individuals and organizations find new and innovative ways to share information with others. The Web was developed in 1989 at the European Laboratory for Particle Physics (CERN) in Geneva, Switzerland by a computer scientist who saw a need for physicists to be able to communicate with colleagues about their work while it was ongoing rather than waiting until a project was finished. To make this *real time* communications possible, he wanted to create an interconnected *web* of documents that would allow a reader to *jump* between documents virtually at will.

To do this, he turned to a concept known as **hypertext**, which is defined as a *method of linking related information in which there is no hierarchy or menu system.* In terms of documents, hypertext involves reading one document on the computer screen, finding a keyword of interest, clicking on that keyword with your mouse, and automatically being switched to another document that provides more information on that keyword. That new document can then be linked to other documents via hypertext which are then linked to other documents and so on to create a web of documents.

With hypertext, a user can navigate throughout a document following predefined links. For example, if you were reading a hypertext version of a computer science text and came upon a reference to the Windows operating system that is indicated as a hypertext link, you could click on this keyword and be shown another page that discusses Windows in more detail. You could then jump to a related discussion on using the mouse to make on-screen selections. From there, you might wish to jump to some other reference that interests you. It is the author's responsibility to anticipate links that readers may want to pursue within a document or to another document. So, readers are restricted to the paths created by a document's author. The World Wide Web is based on this concept of hypertext, where documents are located on computers around the world and hypertext links are denoted in Web documents. Figure 1-4 shows how hypertext works for documents.

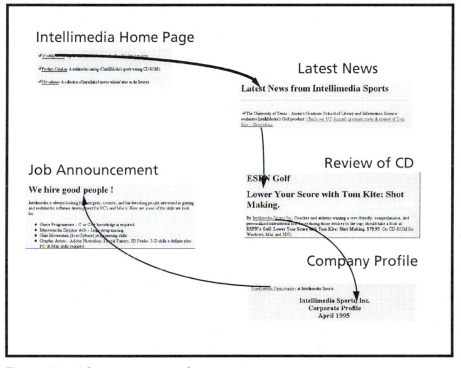

Figure 1-4. A hypertext example

While new to many computer users, hypertext actually predates the use of computers. The original notion was proposed by President Franklin D. Roosevelt's science advisor, Vannevar Bush, in a 1945 *Atlantic* magazine article entitled, "As We May Think." Twenty years later, computer visionary Ted Nelson coined the term *hypertext*. However, hypertext remained a largely hidden concept until Apple released its HyperCard hypertext software system in 1987 for use on the Macintosh. If you have used the Microsoft Windows Help system, then you have already used hypertext to jump to other help screens by clicking on a highlighted keyword.

Internet publishing may replace traditional media

If a Goldman Sachs & Co. report is correct, traditional publications such as newspapers and magazines may be hurt by Internet publishing. For example, the explosive growth of the Internet and the World Wide Web may limit the expansion of the $48 billion newspaper industry to "single digits," far slower than in the past. This same report expects Internet use to triple to 27 million by 1997, with 25 percent of U.S. households having access. Web use is expected to reach 9 million by the end of 1995. The report suggests that newspapers and magazines will lose many readers because they can find the same information more cheaply and easily using computers. The Goldman Sachs report also predicts that majors advertisers in traditional print media such as the *Wall Street Journal* and *Newsweek* will shift to the Internet because it provides more specialized information.

To counteract this move away from print media and to recapture their readership, publications are aggressively going online. Many newspapers are forming alliances to share resources and to make much of their news available for home computers. The New Century Network, which includes over 200 daily newspapers and reaches 25 million American households, will allow computer users to move around member newspapers on the Internet. Another example is Access Atlanta, an online service which allows Prodigy subscribers to read articles from the *Atlanta Journal-Constitution* or to search classified advertisements.

Adapted from: Internet will hurt traditional publications, brokerage report predicts. *Atlanta Journal-Constitution*. August 13, 1995; G: 8.

Client/ server software

The Web is a network of computers running two types of applications: server software and client software. A **server** is a computer running an application that manages a data store containing files of text, images, video clips, and sound. Server computers are set up by individuals and organizations that want to share their information. A **client** is a personal computer running an application that can access data on a server and display it.

A client and server combination are a dynamic duo. They create a short-term partnership to satisfy a person's need for information. A client initiates the partnership by sending a request to a server for certain information. The server responds by retrieving the information from its disk and then transmitting it to the client. On receiving the data, the client formats the information for display. When preparing information for display, the client processes formatting instructions included in the file retrieved from the server. For example, assume that the creator of a document stored on a server has decided a certain phrase should appear in bold when displayed. The server cannot store the data in bold format, however. Instead, it has to store the data with some codes or tags to indicate which text will be in bold when displayed. For instance, the following character string stored on a server:

```
The <B>World Wide Web</B> is a new way of doing busi-
ness.
```

will be displayed by the client as

The **World Wide Web** is a new way of doing business.

because the client interprets the tag "<B>" as turn *on* bolding and the tag "</B>" as turn *off* bolding. This process is shown in Figure 1-5.

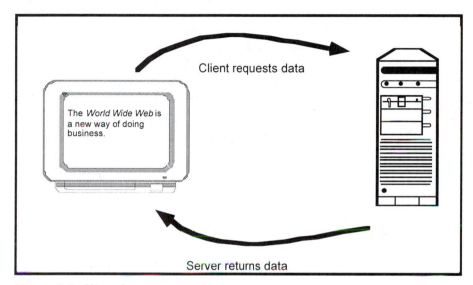

Figure 1-5. Client/server operation

A server can also store **multimedia files,** that is, digitized images, videos, and sound. When a client retrieves these data formats, it converts them into appropriate human recognizable data. Thus, a client would convert a digitized sound file back to human speech or music (and, if we could digitize smells, a client could also reproduce those).

Each of the many servers on the Web has a unique address so that clients can specify where to find requested data. For instance, http://white-house.gov is the address of a server for the Clinton White House. Addresses will be discussed in more detail in Chapter 2.

Flexibility is a great benefit of client/server computing. Servers and clients can run on a wide variety of operating systems. Because clients and servers are set up to interact using a well-defined set of rules, any Web client can request data from any Web server. Hence, client software running under Windows on a compatible PC can successfully access data on a Macintosh server.

The MBone—the future of the Internet?

Although the Internet is now being used to send text, graphics and even audio around the world, video is a problem because of the large amount of bandwidth required for real time transmission. While it is possible to send small amounts of black and white video at slow rates over the Internet via a system called CU-SeeMe (1/16 screen at 5 frames per second versus full screen at 30 frames per second for television), true interactive video over the Internet is not yet possible. However, a new subset of the Internet called the MBone is being developed that might lead to TV quality interactive video. In fact, well over 100 events, including space shuttle missions and two songs from the Dallas stop on the Rolling Stones' "Voodoo Lounge" concert tour, have been broadcast over the MBone. In a medical application of the MBone, approximately 100 doctors in Great Britain and Sweden were able to view an operation in San Francisco and ask questions about it.

The **MBone** (for *Multicast Backbone*) is the brainchild of some computer scientists who were seeking ways to share text, images, and sketches. Rather than broadcasting chunks of information called **packets** from a source to a single destination (so-called *unicasting*), the MBone delivers each packet of information from the source to each requesting destination. Connecting to the MBone is not easy; it requires a powerful computer linked to a high-speed communications link. It is also a voracious consumer of bandwidth and broadcasts over it can slow down the entire Internet. For this reason, it is currently confined to universities and computer research labs, although researchers say that over the next five to ten years, the MBone will become an important part of the Internet.

Adapted from: Hafner, K. The Mbone: can't you hear it knocking? *Newsweek*. December 5, 1994: 86.

Using a browser with the Web

On the Web, the client software is called a **browser**, which can be used to fetch and read documents on screen and print them, jump to other documents via hypertext, view images, and listen to audio files. Web browsers use a **graphical user interface (GUI)** like that of Microsoft Windows or the Apple Macintosh. With a GUI-based Web browser, you can perform various operations simply by pointing at menu selections or icons representing operations and clicking the mouse button—so called **point and click operations**. For example, you can use a browser to navigate the Web by pointing at a hypertext link in the current document and clicking on it. This operation causes the linked document, image file, or audio file to be fetched from a distant computer and displayed or played on the local computer. While not a point and click operation, you can also enter an address to retrieve a desired document or file.

There are a large number of browsers currently available for working on the Web using a PC or Macintosh computer. The two most popular Web browsers are Mosaic and Netscape Navigator. While there is a charge for some of these browsers, most of them are available free of charge from various locations on the Internet. Figure 1-6 shows a popular GUI-based Web browser, Netscape Navigator, in action.

Figure 1-6. GUI Web browser in action

Web pages   The primary purpose of a Web browser is to retrieve electronic documents from Web servers and to display them on a client computer. This electronic document, called a **page**, contains text and hypertext links to multimedia elements and other pages that are stored on server computers. In addition to being electronic rather than physical, Web pages are different from pages in a book or magazine in other ways. For example, while the amount of information on a physical page is restricted to the size of the paper page, a Web page can extend beyond that shown on the screen. Table 1-2 shows the differences between electronic Web pages and physical pages.

Web users can access and display pages using their browser. In many ways, pages are the heart of the Web since they provide users with the information that is unique to the Web. The browser in Figure 1-6 is shown displaying the Web page for this textbook. In addition to displaying text documents,

Table 1-2: Differences between Web pages and physical pages

Characteristic	Web page	Physical page
Form	Electronic	Ink on a paper page
Amount of information	Can extend beyond a single screen	Restricted to one piece of paper
Types of information	Can include text, images, audio, and video information	Restricted to text and images
Links to other pages	Can be linked to an unlimited number of Web pages through hypertext	Can be linked only through a separate index
Creation	Can be created through a markup language and saved to a computer	Can be created using a word processor, desktop publishing, and laser printer

a browser can display graphics and photos and play music and video clips directly without first having to switch to different software packages for each element. When you select a hypertext link to one of these elements, the browser executes helper software which works with that type of multimedia. Figure 1-7 shows a photographic image displayed by a Web browser

Many individuals, companies, and organizations have created Web pages that contain information about themselves and their activities, and more pages are added to the Web every day. There are now numerous services whose sole purpose is to track Web pages and to make their addresses available to Web users. An interesting business application on the Web is discussed in the next section. Other applications will be discussed as we proceed.

While the primary purpose of a browser is to retrieve and display Web pages, it also can be used for five other Internet operations: e-mail, FTP, Telnet, Gopher, and newsgroups. For example, with a Web browser, a user can use FTP to access and retrieve (download) an extensive amount of free software that is available on the Internet. This software has been placed on server computers specifically for downloading by Internet users.

The revolution in business

At the beginning of this chapter, we introduced you to the concept that before businesses can effect meaningful change, they must destroy their current practices or the competitive world will do it for them. No longer is evolutionary change acceptable. Companies must make revolutionary changes to take full advantage of the information technology now available. There are two basic principles of data that you must understand in order to comprehend the forces impelling this revolution: codification and distribution.

Codification describes an organized method for storing data in a computer system. Initially, only alphabetic characters, numbers, and special characters were coded. For example, in ASCII, a popular coding system, each character is represented by a unique 8-bit code. More recently, codification has been extended to include multimedia objects such as images, video, and

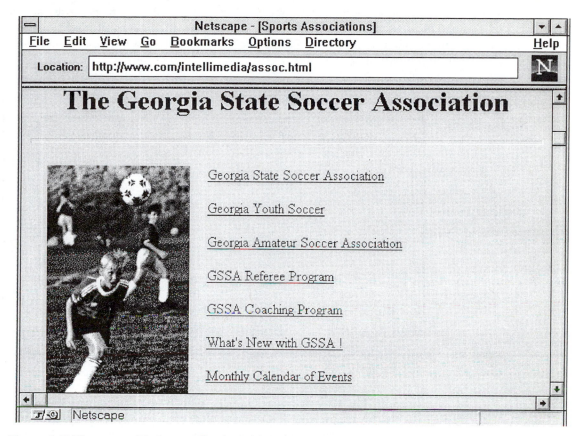

Figure 1-7. Photographic image displayed by a Web browser

audio. Thus, on a computer you can store photos of people, videos of a space shuttle blast-off, and a sound clip from a CD.

Distribution describes how widely information is shared. Several technologies have enabled widespread sharing of information: fiber optics, compression, and networks. Fiber optic cable, with its high communication capacity and low cost, means vast quantities of information can be transported inexpensively. Compression methods, which permit the size of large files to be substantially reduced, make it feasible to transport multimedia objects electronically. Finally, the development of local and wide area networks has created the infrastructure for linking all computers in the world. The combination of these three technologies has made possible the widespread distribution of information.

Figure 1-8 shows that many classes of information systems can be conveniently described by the interaction of codification and distribution where codification goes from low (character only) to high (multimedia) and distribution ranges from local to global. A management information system (MIS) is typically a firm-wide system that provides character-based reports to managers. An MIS falls in the bottom left corner because of its low level of codification (character only) and low distribution (internal to a firm). An executive information system (EIS) is an extension of the MIS idea to meet the special needs of senior executives. Since many EISs include multimedia features (such as charts), they have a high level of codification, but they remain local to an organization.

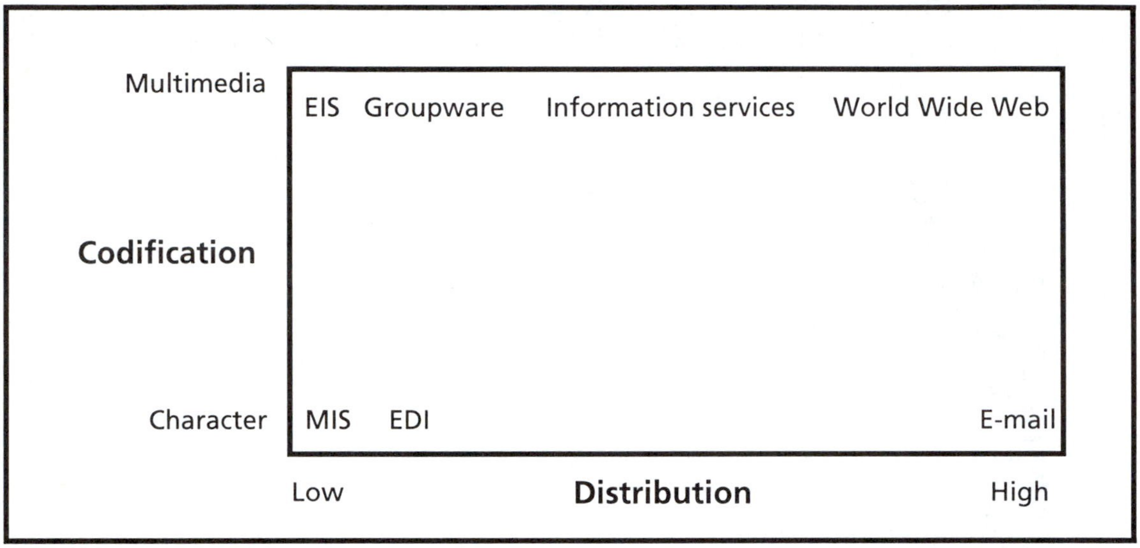

Figure 1-8. Codification and distribution

Electronic data interchange (EDI), character-based electronic communication between trading partners, provides wider information distribution than an MIS because it extends beyond the boundary of one company. It is e-mail, however, that supports the widest distribution of character-based information. The Internet permits widespread global text communication between any two or more people with Internet access—which currently includes tens of millions people.

Groupware, and Lotus Notes in particular, is a step forward in the wider distribution of multimedia. Some Notes applications span several organizations. Information services, such as America Online, CompuServe, and Prodigy, provide an even wider distribution of multimedia information. For example, America Online offers hundreds of interactive information services to its millions of subscribers.

The Web, with its tens of thousands of servers accessible by tens of millions of people, is larger than any commercial information service. Furthermore, nearly all commercial services have embraced the Web by offering connections to it. There are other facets of the Web that make it substantially different from commercial services. The Web is a decentralized network—it is very easy for new Web services to be connected and they do not need the approval of a central authority. The Web is global—a Brazilian consumer can order fish from an Icelandic salmon merchant. The Web has spawned a high degree of entrepreneurial, innovative activity. The combined intelligence of millions of people is creating a highly fertile forum for information.

Because the Web supports a new class of information system—wide distribution of multimedia—and because it is a breeding ground for innovation, we believe that it represents a business revolution. Businesses are discovering that the Web is a new technology for marketing and delivering products and services. As companies exploit this new technology, the competitive forces of free markets and private enterprise will power tremendous change in business. Already, for instance, some catalog companies have discovered that Web ordering is one-third the cost of traditional phone ordering. Businesses have found that they can distribute information to customers in minutes instead of days. There is a large-scale project in Silicon Valley to facilitate electronic commerce between high technology firms. These few examples, and you will discover many more in this book, foretell tremendous change.

Look back at Figure 1-8 and contemplate the change that occurred when an organization introduced an MIS, EDI, or e-mail. Now, speculate about what will happen when we move to the right-top corner of the information codification-distribution grid. We trust you are convinced that we are about to commence a business revolution. Now is the time for you to develop the skills to be an active player in this revolution.

Commerce on the Web

As noted above, commerce on the Web is becoming big business. In this book, we will use four commercial Web sites to demonstrate this trend. These four sites are:

✤ Intellimedia Sports, Inc.

✤ Rhebokskloof Winery

✤ Alberto's Nightclub

✤ Jimmy Buffett's Margaritaville

First, let's take a brief look at the four companies whose Web sites we will use to demonstrate commerce on the Web.

Located in Atlanta, Georgia, Intellimedia Sports specializes in CD-ROMs that provide multimedia instruction in sports including baseball, tennis, golf, and fly fishing. These CD-ROMs use the full range of multimedia elements in their instruction including full-motion video, sound, graphics, animation, and text. To publicize their products, Intellimedia Sports has created a Web page for which the initial or "home" page is shown in Figure 1-9. Note the use of graphics on this page.

Rhebokskloof Estate is found at the northern end of the Paarl Valley in one of South Africa's best wine-producing areas. Virtual visitors can tour the winery, visit the wineshop, and check out the three restaurants on the estate. We recommend the Cape Dutch Homestead if you would like to sample the local fare. You can also read about the several red and white wines offered for sale and even place an order.

Experience the atmosphere and excitement of Alberto's nightclub. The Mountain View, California nightclub provides live music and shows. Learn about the rhythms of the Salsa, and check out the dance instructors—Alex and Nicole.

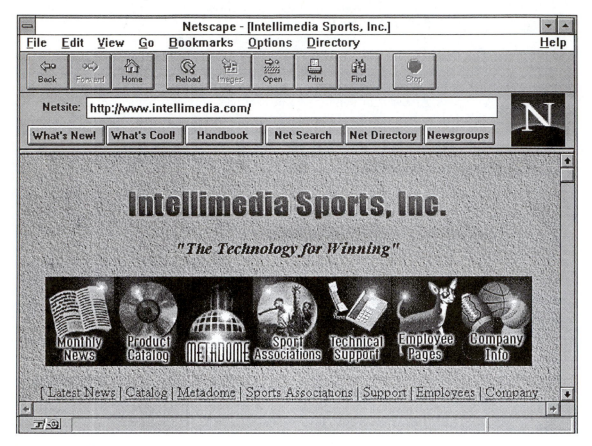

Figure 1-9. The Intellimedia Sports home page

For many fans around the world, Jimmy Buffett's music epitomizes a lifestyle which they would like attain. Now, parrotheads, as Buffett's fans like to be called, have their own Web page. Sponsored by Jimmy Buffett's Margaritaville, a store in Key West, Florida, this page has many features including an information source called the Coconut Telegraph, a list of records under Jimmy's own Margaritaville label, a list of tour dates, a section devoted to the environment, and a section for ordering a wide variety of Jimmy Buffett wearing apparel using an electronic order form.

A roadmap to this book

The five upcoming chapters should be read sequentially. Chapter 2 discusses the use of browsers to access the Web while Chapter 3 covers the use of a specific browser, Netscape, in detail. Chapter 4 covers the design and construction of home pages, and Chapter 5 discusses using a browser to access other types of information on the Internet. Finally, Chapter 6 returns to the topic of commerce on the Web, discussing which companies should use the Web for commerce and how they should use it.

A unique feature of this systematic ordering is that the reader is able to go through the first four chapters without requiring access to remote sites on the

Web. To do this, the Netscape Navigator browser is used to access local Web pages stored on a hard disk. Also, a text editor is used to create home pages that are stored on a floppy disk. If the reader has access to the Web, then in Chapter 5, Netscape can be used to access various Web pages, carry out search operations, and to access Internet operations.

Key terms and concepts

browser
centralized network
client
codification
computer
computer network
decentralized network
distribution
download
e-mail
FTP (File Transfer Protocol)
Gopher
graphical user interface (GUI)
hypertext

Internet
Internet operations
Internet provider
local mode
modem
multimedia files
page
point and click operations
protocol
server
TCP/IP
USENET newsgroups
World Wide Web
Web

Exercises

1. What is the principle of creative destruction? What does it have to do with business and industry?
2. Why is the Internet referred to as a "network of networks?"
3. What is a protocol? What does it have to do with the Internet?
4. What is TCP/IP? Why do we relate the Internet the to U.S. interstate highway system?
5. Discuss common ways that users have access to the Internet. Which method(s) do you have?
6. List the important applications of the Internet. Which have you already used?
7. What does hypertext have to do with the World Wide Web? What type of software is necessary to be able to use the Web?
8. What type of interface do browsers offer the user?
9. What is hypertext? How is it implemented on a browser?
10. What type of information is available on the Web? What is a Web page?
11. What are some of the differences between a Web page and a physical page?
12. What is a client? A server? What do they have to do with the Web?

13. What is a browser? What does it have to do with multimedia?
14. What is the primary purpose of a browser?
15. What are codification and distribution? What do they have to do with types of information systems?

2 Introduction to Browsers

Objectives

After completing this chapter, you will be able to:

❖ discuss the use of browsers to access the Web;

❖ understand Internet addresses and URLs;

❖ discuss the types of files that are a part of a Web page;

❖ describe key operations than can be performed with a browser;

❖ access Netscape in a Windows system;

❖ use Netscape to access a Web page.

Introduction

As discussed in Chapter 1, the Web is the newest and fastest growing part of the Internet with the number of networks connected to it doubling each year for the past 5 years. In March 1995, the volume of traffic over the Web surpassed that of e-mail, the previous volume leader. Dr. Larry Smarr, Director of the National Center for Supercomputer Applications (NCSA), has predicted that by the year 2000, close to *1 billion* people will have personal computers (up from less than 200 million in 1995) and that virtually all of these people will be on the Web.[1] He went further and stated that those connected will be reading documents available on the Web and publishing information themselves. While Dr. Smarr's prediction *may* be overly optimistic, undoubtedly we are moving into a true *information age* and the Web is the catalyst that is making this move possi-

---

1. Larry L. Smarr, "The creation of cyberspace: how the Internet will change your life," The University of Georgia, May 3, 1995.

ble. For business, the Web is opening up new horizons that had not been previously considered. For those companies willing to make the metamorphosis, the Web will bring very positive results.

Recall from Chapter 1 that the Web is a **client/server network** on which server computers make documents available to users running client software on their personal computers. The client software that is used to access, display, save, and print the documents stored on servers located anywhere in the world is called a **browser**. It is so named because this software allows the user to "browse" the many Web servers around the world. Recall also, that these are not just ordinary sequential text documents; rather, the documents available on Web servers make wide use of both hypertext and multimedia. Figure 2-1 shows how a browser displays a document with information on one of the companies we discussed in Chapter 1, Intellimedia Sports, Inc.

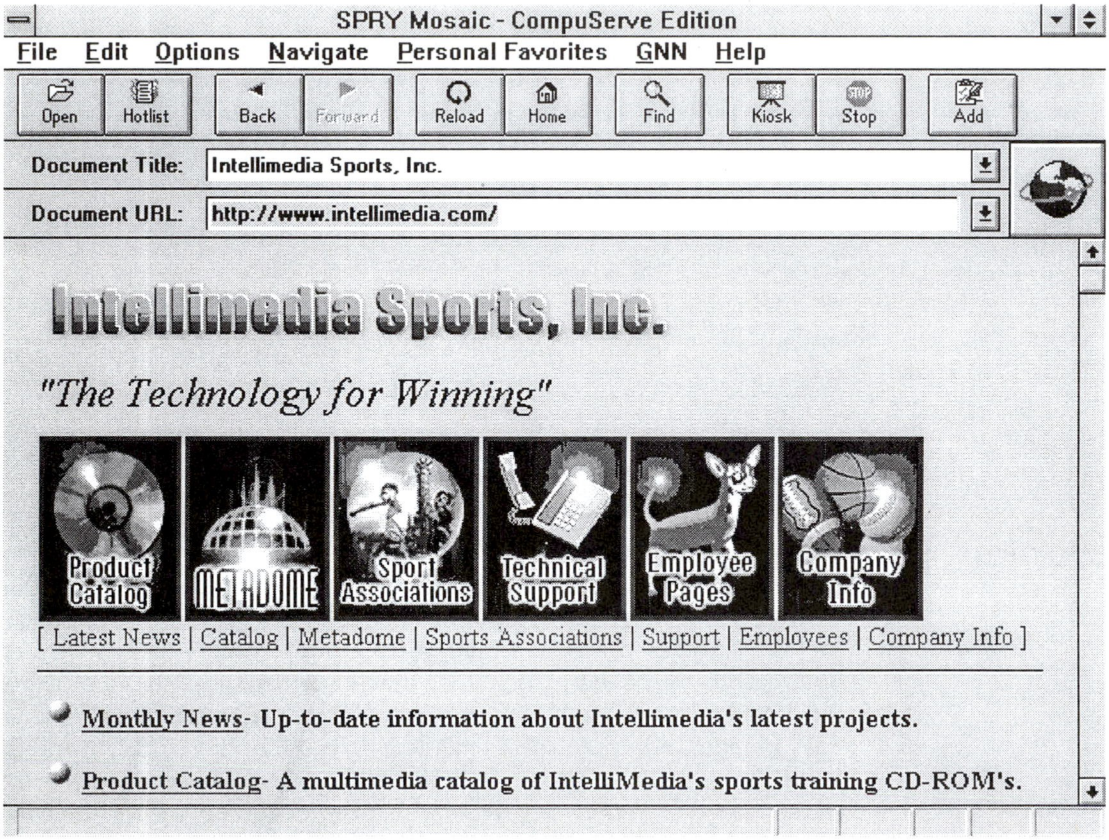

Figure 2-1. Intellimedia Sports, Inc. document

Hypertext, a non-sequential method of linking related information, means you can jump from document to document by following a trail of hyperlinks that represent areas of interest to you. Another element of Web documents that distinguishes them is the wide use of **multimedia**; that is, an interactive combination of text, graphics, animation, images, audio, and video displayed by and under the control of a personal computer. On the Web, multimedia makes documents more interesting and informative than a book or magazine. When you view a Web document, you can see a picture or graphic element, hear an audio clip or even view a video clip that provides additional information on the text in the document. In many Web documents, hypertext and multimedia are combined to create **hypermedia**. With hypermedia, a user can click on a graphic image and hear an audio clip or click on a word in the document and see an animation. In the case of the Web document shown in Figure 2-1, the hypertext links are represented by underlined words or phrases and the graphical and photographic images represent a form of multimedia.

More on browsers

A key element that has enabled the Web to become such a popular vehicle for sharing information is the graphical browser client software like Netscape and Mosaic. Graphical browsers make it easy for users to find and display hypermedia Web documents. While there are non-graphical browsers like Lynx, when we refer to "browsers" in the future, we are referring to graphical browsers. Without them, it is extremely doubtful that the Web would have become as popular as it is now.

To understand the impact of Web browsers, consider the effect they have had on the growth of traffic on the Internet. After 15 years of relative obscurity as a network used primarily by defense researchers, the Internet started to grow in 1986 when the National Science Foundation funded the first high-speed communications "backbone" linkage between five supercomputer centers across the country. This allowed many universities to be linked into the Internet resulting in a significant growth in traffic over the network. This growth was increased in 1992 when commercial organizations were also allowed to link into and use the Internet. The real growth in the Internet has occurred since 1993 when the first widely available graphical browser, Mosaic, allowed people to explore the World Wide Web. For example, the Internet traffic measured at the National Center for Supercomputer Applications has increased by a factor of *100,000* since the introduction of Mosaic in 1993.[2] Figure 2-2 shows the growth of the Internet in terms of number of networks connected to it.

Problems with the Internet

To understand why browsers have had such a dramatic impact, you need to know that prior to the introduction of the Web and browsers, many people found the Internet difficult to use. There were several reasons for this, including the fact that the Internet was (and still is) based primarily on the computers running the Unix operating system, it required separate software packages for each application, and it was primarily oriented toward displaying text and numbers. These difficulties are summarized in Table 2-1.

---

2. Ibid.

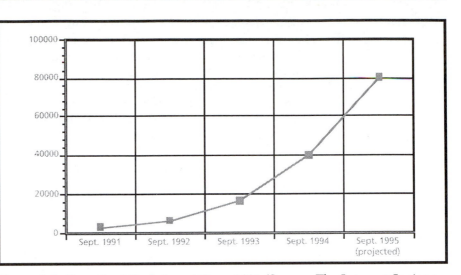

Figure 2-2. Growth of the Internet Since 1991 (Source: The Internet Society, Reston, Virginia)

Table 2-1: Difficulties with the Internet

Problem
Text-oriented Unix operating system
Separate software packages
Orientation toward text and numbers

In the first case, while Unix is a very powerful operating system for working with networks of computers, it is anything but "user friendly!" In fact, unless a graphical user interface such as X-Windows is used, Unix requires a knowledge of various commands that must be typed into the computer in the same way that DOS commands are entered. While Unix commands were not a problem for many early users of the Internet, it did discourage widespread use. For example, to download a file from another computer, you had to use appropriate commands to navigate the various directories to find the file, enter a command to define the file as being a text or binary (machine language) file, and then use the appropriate command (GET) to download the file to your computer. (A typical screen and the required FTP commands to download a file from a Unix system are shown in Figure 2-3). While there are some Windows-based and Macintosh applications that allow the use of a point-and-click interface, other Unix-based Internet software applications still require a command line interface.

A second problem with using the Internet is that users need a separate program or client for each of the applications on the Internet. Recall from Chapter 1 that these applications include **FTP, e-mail, Telnet, USENET newsgroups** (or simply **News**), and **Gopher.**

```
BootP: RFC1048 Style BootP Packet Received
BootP: Subnet is 255.255.0.0
BootP: Adding Gateway number 1 IP 128.192.1.1
BootP: Adding Nameserver number 1 IP 128.192.1.9
BootP: This Clients Name is pmckeown
Domain looking for www.cba.uga.edu
220 Peter's Macintosh FTP daemon v2.3.0 (Unregistered) awaits your command.
Username: telecom
331 Password required.
Password:
    either the same folder as FTPd or the FTPd Preferences   159

    folder in the Preferences folder, and will be displayed to
    any user that does not have a personal Startup message
    when they log in.
hen they log in.
oes not have a personal Startup messageftp> dir
230 User logged in to 2 volumes, directory is "/Pub".
200 PORT command successful.
drwxrwxr-x                folder      36 Aug 10 14:29 MacGames
drwxrwxrwx                folder      44 Aug 14 09:42 WWW
Transferred 123 bytes in 0 seconds (0.120 Kbytes/sec)
150 ASCII transfer started.
226 Transfer complete.
ftp>
```

Figure 2-3. Typical Unix FTP interaction

Before the creation of Web browsers, no single software program could handle all these applications. This meant that separate software applications had to be installed on each computer and users had to learn a variety of commands to use the individual applications.

Finally, because Unix-based Internet was primarily text-based, it was directed at displaying text and numbers, not graphics or photos or playing music or videos. While it was (and still is) possible to download files containing photos or music from Internet computers, it was not possible to play them on the same software that was used for downloading. It was necessary to shift to another piece of software to view the photo or to play the music file.

Web browsers solve all of these Internet problems. Table 2-2 shows the same problems with the Internet that were shown in Table 2-1 plus the solutions provided by Web browsers. A browser with its graphical interface is easy to use with no need to learn arcane Unix commands. Browsers are also capable of carrying out almost all applications mentioned previously, thereby eliminating the need for multiple software packages. (The one exception to this is that you can send but *not* receive e-mail, though Netscape 2.0 will add support for receipt of mail). Finally, browsers can both download and display images as well as play audio and video files. By solving these Internet problems, Web browsers have made it easy and fun for many more people to have access to the virtually unlimited amount of information that is available on the Internet.

Table 2-2: Web browser solutions to Internet problems

Problem	Web browser solution
Unix operating system	Easy-to-use GUI software
Separate software packages	Browser does it all (except for incoming e-mail
Orientation toward text and numbers	Browser handles multimedia as well as text

History of browsers

As mentioned in Chapter 1, the Web was developed at CERN in Switzerland in 1989. The first browsers were text-based packages that ran only on Unix machines. A hypertext link is selected by entering a number which retrieves a corresponding document. While text-based browsers such as Lynx are still used on text-only networks, they have been rapidly eclipsed by graphical browsers.

Realizing a trend in personal computers toward graphical interfaces on Windows for compatible PCs and Macintosh computers, a group of students at the University of Illinois working at the National Center for Supercomputer Applications (NCSA) began to create a graphical browser. Led by an undergraduate, this group developed a graphical browser called *Mosaic*. First released in February 1993 for Unix-based workstations, Mosaic was also available for Macintosh and Windows-based machines by the fall of 1993. Because Mosaic was developed by a publicly-funded research facility, it was made available to Internet users free of charge. The meteoric growth of the Web discussed earlier and shown in Figure 2-2 was a direct result of the wide availability of free browser software. This policy of freely giving away browsers has continued to be followed for non-commercial users for revised versions of Mosaic and for other browsers. (See Figure 2-1 for an example of the Mosaic browser.)

While not the first graphical browser, the development of Mosaic is considered by many to be the key event that led to the widespread use of the Web. A December 1993 article in the *New York Times* referred to Mosaic as the "killer application of the Internet," however, like other "killer apps" such as the VisiCalc spreadsheet and the dBASE database management software, which initially controlled their respective markets, Mosaic has generated competition. In this case, Mosaic's primary developer, Marc Andreeson, and some of his colleagues left NCSA and joined computer industry executives to form a company dedicated to creating a better browser. *Netscape Navigator*, the result of this work, was released in fall 1994. As with Mosaic, Netscape is available free of charge to non-commercial users. The company, Netscape Communications, Inc., generates revenue by selling the server software necessary to distribute Web documents as well as other software needed to publish Web documents.

Netscape offers many improvements over the original Mosaic and has become the most popular browser in use today. However, since both Compuserve and Microsoft have licensed versions of Mosaic, there should be healthy competition between the two browsers for the foreseeable future. We will demonstrate the use of browsers with Netscape in this chapter

Using Browsers

Information is available on the Web primarily as documents called Web pages. As mentioned in Chapter 1, a **Web page** is a special type of document that contains hypertext links to other documents or to various multimedia elements. Some multimedia elements like graphics and images are actually displayed on the Web page. Others are played separately from the Web page. Web pages are retrieved from Internet server computers commonly referred to as **Web sites**. The first page you encounter when you visit a Web site is the **home page,** from which you can explore other Web pages that have been linked to it. For example, the Web page shown earlier in Figure 2-1 is the home page for information on Intellimedia Sports, Inc. We have shown this same home page again in Figure 2-4. Only, this time the home page is shown in the Netscape browser instead of the Mosaic browser.

Web pages are created using a set of special tags defined by the **Hypertext Markup Language (HTML)**. HTML is used to create the format of the Web pages in terms of features such as boldfacing, underlining, and sizes of headings. HTML is also used to create the links between Web pages and between Web pages and multimedia elements. HTML is discussed in detail in Chapter 4.

Browser elements

In looking at Figure 2-4, the **menu bar** at the top of the screen is used to execute various commands, as are the various **toolbar buttons** immediately beneath the menu bar. A text box contains the **Web page address**, which is the Internet address that is used to retrieve this Web page. Below the Web page address are the **directory buttons** that provide links to interesting and helpful pages. The Web page itself is displayed in the **main screen.** Note that some words or phrases are underlined in the Web page. These underlined elements are the clickable **hypertext links.** When you move the pointer to a clickable link, the pointer changes to a pointing finger and the address of that link is shown at the bottom of the browser screen (illustrated in Figure 2-5)

Clicking on a link enables you to jump from the current Web page to other pages, multimedia elements, or other Web resources. (The clickable links are also in color, which you cannot see on this black-and-white page.) They also can be links to other parts of the current document. These latter links act like a "hyper table of contents" that allow you to go to any other part of the document by simply clicking on the link. Icons or images also can be used as hypertext links, which are indicated by a colored border. Clicking on such an icon or image will shift control to another home page, a different section of the current home page, or a multimedia element. Figure 2-6 shows the result of clicking on the "Latest News" hypertext link in the Intellimedia Sports home page. Note that there is another link to a page created by a completely different organization. It is not unusual for creators to link their pages to other related pages in different organizations.

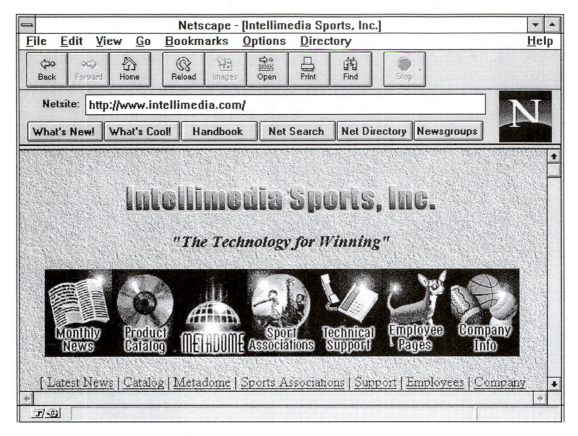

Figure 2-4. Home page for Intellimedia Sports, Inc.

Scroll bars on the right side and bottom of the main screen allow you to move to parts of the Web page that are not currently on the screen. While we refer to documents on the Web as "pages," they are usually much longer than a single page of information. For that reason, you need to use the vertical scroll bar to move up and down the Web page.

Two colors distinguish the hypertext links, often blue and purple. The blue links correspond to Web pages or parts of the same page that have not yet been visited while the purple links correspond to Web pages that have been visited recently. These distinguishing colors are very useful when you jump from Web page to Web page and cannot always remember which links have been followed.

You will also note the numerous **graphic elements** in Figure 2-4. These are examples of multimedia elements. While not shown in this figure, other home pages might also have audio or video elements that can be played by clicking on an icon. The most famous audio file in a Web home page is the sound of Socks, the First Family's cat, meowing in the White House home page.

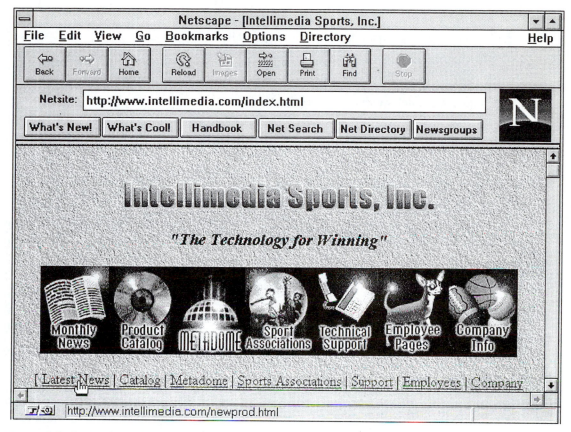

Figure 2-5. A clickable hypertext link

Browser operations

With a browser, you can perform several key operations to access the information that is available on the Internet. These operations include:

❖ retrieving a home page;

❖ connecting to other Web pages via hypertext links;

❖ navigating among Web pages;

❖ retrieving previously viewed Web pages;

❖ searching for interesting Web Pages;

❖ saving and printing Web pages;

❖ using e-mail, forms, and maps.

We will discuss the first operation—retrieving a home page—in some detail. We will then briefly discuss each of the other operations. Finally, we will discuss how to access Netscape and use it to retrieve a home page and then connect to another Web page. In Chapter 3, we will show how to use Netscape to carry out each operation. In Chapter 5, we will discuss a variety of other browser operations.

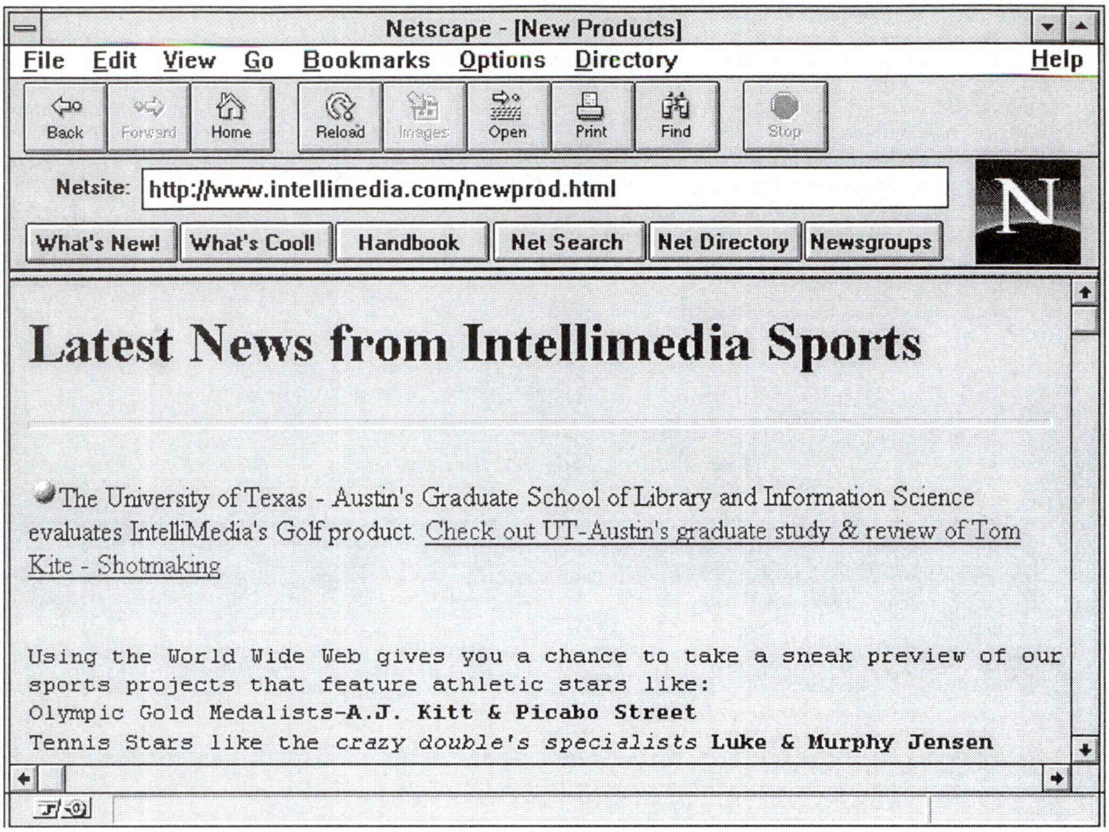

Figure 2-6. The result of clicking a hypertext link

Because graphical browsers run under Microsoft Windows on IBM-compatible PCs, on Apple Macintosh computers, or on X-Windows Unix workstations, a graphical user interface (GUI) is used to work with them. A mouse or trackball can be used to select options from menus or to click on buttons to perform browser operations.

Retrieving a home page

A Web home page is accessed by an address. In Web terminology, the address of a home page is referred to as its **URL** (for **Uniform Resource Locator**.) It is so named because a URL is a standard means of consistently locating Web pages or other resources no matter where they are stored on the Internet. For example, the URL of the Intellimedia Sports home page shown in Figure 2-4 is

http://www.intellimedia.com/index.html

Like every URL, this one has four parts: the protocol, the Internet address of the server computer on which the desired resource is located, the port number (optional), and the path of the resource. Three parts of the Intellimedia address (which does not have a port number) are shown in Figure 2-7

http://www.intellimedia.com/index.html

Protocol   Server address   Path of the resource

Figure 2-7. Parts of a URL

In computer terminology, a **protocol** is a set of rules that defines how computers will communicate. For Web resources, the protocol (also called the **service resource**) defines the type of resource being retrieved. The Web page resource is defined by the letters **http**, which stands for **Hypertext Transfer Protocol**. In addition to home page documents, some of the other allowable protocols include file, telnet, ftp, gopher, and mailto. Table 2-3 shows these protocols (service resources) and their purpose. A very important aspect of these protocols is that they are *all* in lower case, for example, ftp. When included in a URL, a protocol must be entered in this fashion.

Table 2-3: Web protocols

Protocol	Purpose
http	Retrieve a Web page
file	Retrieve a file on a local disk
telnet	Log onto a computer connected to the Internet
ftp	Retrieve a file from an FTP server
gopher	Search for a document on a Gopher server
mailto	Send outgoing e-mail

The **server address** gives the address of the computer on which the resource is stored. Just as there is a system to city and street addresses and telephone numbers, there is a system for Internet addresses. A server address is composed of two to five words, separated by periods, that define the name of the computer, the type of organization, and, possibly, the country of origin. In our example, www is the name of the server computer and com is the type of organization.

The third part of the URL is the **port number,** which indicates an internal address within the server. It is shown as a colon (:) followed by a number immediately after the organization or country code. For example, an address that does have a port number is the URL for the British Broadcasting System:

http://www.bbcnc.org.uk:80/bbctv/

where the protocol is http, the server name is www.bbcnc.org.uk, and the port number is 80.

The fourth part of the URL is the **path** of the Web resource, which includes the name of the home page file plus any directories or folders in which it is located. In the Intellimedia Sports example, the name of the home page document is index.html. In this case, its home page file, called index.html, is stored in the root directory of the server. The extension html refers to the language used to create a home page. For DOS and Windows-based systems, this extension is shortened to be htm. Because embedded spaces in path names can create problems, an underscore (e.g., White_House) is used to connect words.

Some other URLs are illustrated in Table 2-4. In this case, all URLs describe HTML files because the service component is http.

Table 2-4: Example URLs

URL	Description
http://albertos.com/albertos/	Alberto's nightclub in Mountain View, California
http://www.intellimedia.com/	Intellimedia Sports
http://www.os2.iaccess.za/rhebok/index.htm	Rhebokskloof Winery in South Africa
http://key-west.com/cgibin/var/discover/margaritaville/	Jimmy Buffet's Margaritaville Store located in Key West, Florida
http://www.microsoft.com/pages/ services/jobops/toplevel.htm	Job opportunities at Microsoft
http://www.wiley.com/	John Wiley & Sons.
http://www.whitehouse.gov/White_House/Tours/Welcome.html	A virtual tour of the White House
http://www.arctic.is/Transport/ Icelandair/	Iceland Air
http://www.tansu.com.au/	Telecom Australia, Information Technology Group, Network Systems, Sydney

Observe in Table 2-4 that some paths end with a slash (e.g., albertos/). This indicates that the **default HTML file,** index.html, should be accessed. In the case of Alberto's night club, the URL is interpreted as:

http://albertos.com/albertos/index.html.

Use of index.html is quite common and saves unnecessary typing. It also means that you can often guess the URL of an organization's home page. For example, you would guess correctly if you tried http://www.dell.com/ to access Dell Computer's home page. Another common name for the default file is default.html.

Once a valid address for a resource has been entered, the next step is automatic: the browser software attempts to connect to the server computer at that address and to find the page referenced in the address. If this operation is successful, then the page is displayed on the screen.

Using e-mail and the Web for interactive advertising

When Coors Brewing Company wanted to advertise its new *Zima* beverage aimed at young, well-educated, techno-savvy males, it immediately thought of using the Internet. Coors selected the ModemMedia company to handle the advertising. ModemMedia decided to use e-mail to reach virtually all consumers with modems. But because e-mail broadcasts are usually perceived to be obvious violations of netiquette, ModemMedia decided to publish Zima's e-mail address on the product's packaging in a way that a net-wise consumer would find and use it. E-mail messages to Zima were automatically answered with a message and a GIF image file. The names of newsgroups that were dedicated to the beverage were also published on the packaging to encourage consumers to visit them.

In addition, a Web site (http://www.zima.com), which contains a relatively large amount of information and is fun to visit, was established by ModemMedia. The site was composed of four key elements: a very colorful home page, a consumer information center with a forms feature, a biweekly serial installment starring a fictional character, and the "fridge." This last element, an image map that links nine other information areas, has gained a great deal of attention. Originally perceived as an archive of multimedia utilities, it has now mushroomed to include a huge repository of product images, sound files, icons, consumer postings, pointers to other locations, and more. It is well known as the most comprehensive hot list of bars and restaurants in the United States.

Adapted from: O'Connell, G. M. Net campaign case study. *Internet World.* May, 1995: 57-58.

Retrieving local files

One of the shortcomings of the Web is that it takes a great deal of transmission capacity or **bandwidth** on the Internet, especially when graphics, audio, or video files are being transmitted. The bandwidth of the communications lines that connect a computer or local area network to the Internet are measured in bits per second (bps). For example, many educational institutions are connected to the Internet by T1 lines that transmit approximately 1.5 million bps. However, even the much faster T1 lines can be clogged when an entire class attempts to retrieve Web pages at the same time. In addition, if everyone in the class simultaneously attempted to access the same Web server, the computer could not handle the demand and very few students would be successful in retrieving a page.

To resolve the problems with inadequate bandwidth and overloaded Web servers, we have created **local files** that have been placed on your floppy disk, hard disk, or network file server by your instructor. These local files contain Web pages with graphics just like you would retrieve if you accessed a Web site. To retrieve a Web page stored as a local file on disk, you would use the **file protocol** instead of the http protocol when entering the URL. The form of the file URL is **file:///** plus the local path name. For example, to retrieve the Intellimedia Sports home page from a hard disk (drive c:), you would enter the URL[3] (if the files have been placed on your floppy disk, replace the c: drive designation with a:. If they have been placed on a file server, your instructor will give you the drive designation):

file:///c:\weblearn\IMS\index.htm

When we discuss the use of Netscape later in this chapter and in detail in Chapter 3, we will ask you to use the file protocol to retrieve local Web pages from a floppy drive or hard disk on your local PC. To retrieve the same home page from a Web site, you simply change the local URL to the appropriate remote URL that uses the http protocol. Note: because Web pages are constantly being changed, the Web pages you retrieve from your hard disk may differ from the same Web pages you retrieve from a Web site. However, they will give you a good look at Web pages without using precious Internet bandwidth.

Formatting Web pages

It is important to remember that the text displayed on the screen is actually a simple **text (ASCII) file** that contains only keyboard characters and Hypertext Markup Language (HTML) codes. The browser interprets the text and codes to generate the page that appears in the form that you see. This includes retrieving the images and formatting the page to make the text and images to fit the on-screen window. If the window is small, then the text and images will be formatted differently than if the on-screen window is full-screen. Figure 2-8 shows the same Intellimedia Sports Web page shown earlier as Figure 2-6, now reformatted to fit a smaller window.

Another important aspect about browsers and Web pages is that a page will have a very similar appearance when displayed by the same browser on a compatible PC, a Macintosh, or an X-Windows workstation. You do not have to create different versions of a page for the different types of computers currently in use.

---

3. This assumes you are using a DOS/Windows machine. If you are using a Macintosh, your instructor will provide you with instructions on the drive and folder.

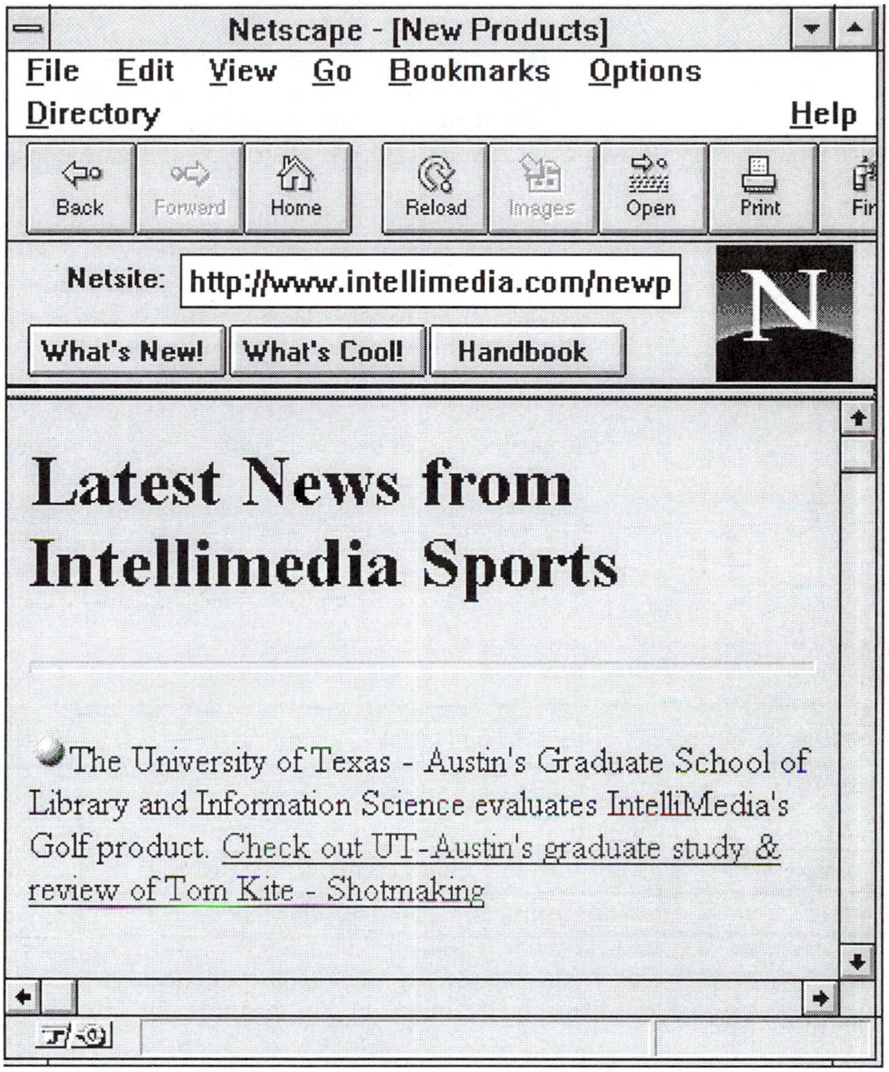

Figure 2-8. A page reformatted into a narrower window

Web page files

Web pages are typically composed of html (hypermedia) files and image files. The html portion of the page is retrieved fairly quickly, but the image files that are linked to the page can take some time to be received from the server. This can especially be true if the page is being received over a modem. For this reason, most browsers offer the capability to display only text, ignoring images when a page is being retrieved. One of the improvements included in Netscape is the capability to scroll down a page and read text elements even while the images are still being received. That way, users do not have to wait for images to be completely received before reading the textual information on the page.

In addition to the html and small image files that are an integral part of Web pages, large image files, audio files, and video files also may be linked to a Web page. While text and small images are automatically displayed when the page is retrieved, audio and video files are usually played "off-line," that is, they are not automatically played when the page is received. Large image files are also often displayed off-line. These images may be a larger version of a small on-line image file or totally separate images.

There are two reasons for this different handling of large images, audio, and video. First, special "helper" software packages are required for playing audio or video files or displaying a large image file. These **helper software** packages are linked to the browser in such a way that they are invoked automatically when the user requests an audio or video file or a large image. Web pages often include an icon that is linked to an image, audio, or video file, that when clicked on, downloads the file and plays or displays it.

The second reason that audio and video files are not usually automatically played or large images displayed is that they are often very large and can take a long time to download from a server computer. To help you understand the sizes of the audio and video files relative to html and image files, we have shown in Table 2-5 the four files along with their file extensions, the size of a typical file in bytes, and typical helper software programs.

Table 2-5: Files in Web pages

Type of File	Extension	Relative Size	Helper Software
HTML	html or htm	1-2 kbytes	Browser
images	gif or jpg	5-500 kbytes per image	LView
audio	au or wav	at least 30 kbytes per second	Wplyany and Naplayer
video	mov or mpg	at least 1.5 Mbytes per second	Quicktime or MPEGPlay

A file size usually accompanies the icon to inform the user of the size of the file to be downloaded. For example, the brief meow sound file for Socks the White House cat[4] is 36 kbytes. This size factor becomes especially important when a file is being downloaded over a modem, since even the fastest modem available today (28,800 bits per second) will take quite a while to download a 100 kbyte file. Some of these problems are being resolved for audio files by a new type of helper software which plays them in "real time," that is, they are played as they are downloaded.

Other browser operations

Once a home or other Web page has been retrieved, you can then use a browser to perform other operations including: linking to other Web pages, navigating among them, retrieving previously viewed Web pages, searching for interesting Web pages, saving and printing Web pages, sending e-mail, filling out forms, and using maps in a Web page.

---

4. http://www.whitehouse.gov

Linking to other web pages

You may link to other Web pages from the current page by simply clicking on a highlighted (underlined and colored) hypertext word or phase. When you click on a hypertext link, the associated Web page is automatically retrieved.

What's in a name

The Internet address of the server computer to which you are attached is an important element of a URL or e-mail address. It tells the Internet where to send your Web page or e-mail. Since you or your organization can choose your own server address to some extent, your server address can tell the on-line world something about you. In a sense, a server address acts like a postal address, vanity license plate, and advertising billboard all rolled into one.

If the server address is so important, just how does an individual or organization obtain one? The answer is very simple: server addresses are available on a first come-first served basis by applying to the Internet Network Information Center (InterNIC) in Virginia. And, until recently, there was no control over the use of company trademarks in server addresses, that is, there was nothing to keep an individual or organization from applying for and receiving a trademark name for their server address. This policy has led to some interesting situations. For example, it was very easy for *Newsday* writer Joshua Quittner to request Mcdonalds.com or for Music Television (MTV) host Adam Curry to obtain MTV.com. However, probably the most publicized case of server address conflict involved the two test preparation companies Princeton Review and Kaplan Education Centers. The Princeton Review president registered kaplan.com as a server address for his company's computer and anyone that logged onto kaplan.com read a comparison of the two companies that heavily favored Princeton Review's products. This case was finally solved when an arbitration panel ruled Kaplan should have its name back. Recently, InterNIC has begun withholding server names that might lead to conflict. By the way, Adam Curry and MTV resolved their conflict by having the server address sold to the music network.

Adapted from: Quittner, J. Writer has Ronald McDonald's name as Internet e-mail address. *The Athens Daily News/Athens Banner-Herald.* October 16, 1994; D:8.

Navigating among web pages

Once you have linked to another Web page from the home page, you can begin navigating among Web pages. Browsers automatically keep up with the URLs of Web pages that have been visited. There are reverse and forward buttons that allow you to move backward and forward through previously visited home pages. There is a history option that will store a partial list of recently visited Web site URLs. You can select a URL from the history list and jump to that page. Finally, there is a home button that sends you back to the "home" Web site that automatically appears on the screen when the browser is accessed.

Remembering home page addresses

Once you have found an interesting Web page, browsers can help you remember its URL. They do this via an operation that goes by various names like "Hotlist" or "Bookmarks." If a URL is saved to a Bookmarks file, it can then be accessed without re-entry. For example, you could save the Intellimedia Sports address in a Bookmarks file and then later select it or some other URL that has been saved. This is true regardless of whether the Web page is retrieved from a Web site or as a local file from disk. While it might seem like Bookmarks and history lists are the same, they are actually quite different. The Bookmarks list is a *static* list that does not change unless you add another bookmark or remove an existing one. Otherwise, it will stay the same from session to session. On the other hand, the history list is *dynamic*, changing as you move around Web pages, and disappears when you exit the browser.

Searching for home pages

An important operation in all browsers is that of searching for home pages that meet some criteria defined by the user. In every case, the browser is not doing the actual searching, but is referring to one of several **search engines** that have been developed by Web users. These search engines go by such names as WebCrawler[5], World Wide Web Worm[6], and Yahoo[7]. Regardless of the name, all of these search programs allow you to enter a word or phrase that is used to search for matching home pages.

Saving or printing retrieved information

Once a Web page has been displayed, all or part of it may be saved to a local file under the page file name or under a name you assign. For example, if you saved the Intellimedia Sports home page on a Windows system, it would be saved on your local disk as index.htm or another name you choose. You can also print this page.

If you opt to save the page to a local file, it is important to remember that the images will *not* be automatically saved along with the Web page text. Since they are separate files, they must be saved separately. This means that if you bring the local file into the browser, you will see only the text. In many cases, however, the text by itself can be very useful to you since it contains much important information as well as all of the hypertext links to other documents. If you retrieved the index.htm file discussed previously, you would only see the text with no images.

Another important aspect of a saved Web page file is that, if it is retrieved into an editor like the DOS editor or Windows Write, you will see the text ver-

---

5. http://webcrawler.com/cgi-bin/WebCrawler/WebQuery.html

6. http://www.cs.colorado.edu/home/mcbryan/WWWW.html

7. http://www.yahoo.com/search.html

```
┌─────────────────────────────────────────────────────────────┐
│ ─                        View Source                          │
├─────────────────────────────────────────────────────────────┤
│ ┌─────────────────────────────────────────────────────────┐▲│
│ │<html>                                                   │ ││
│ │<title>Intellimedia Sports, Inc.</title>                 │ ││
│ │<body>                                                   │ ││
│ │<center><img src="ims.gif"></center>                     │ ││
│ │<center><img src="wavey.gif"></center>                   │ ││
│ │<center><h3><i>"The Technology for Winning"</i></h3></center>│ │
│ │<center><a href="newprod.html><img src="newprod.gif"></a><a href="catlog.html'│
│ │<br>                                                     │ ││
│ │<center>                                                 │ ││
│ │[ <a href="newprod.html">Latest News</a> | <a href="catlog.html">Catalog</a> |│
│ │<p>                                                      │ ││
│ │<hr size=4><br>                                          │ ││
│ │<img src="green-do.gif"><a href="newprod.html"><b>Monthly News</b></a>- Up·│
│ │<img src="green-do.gif"><a href="catlog.html"><b>Product Catalog</b></a>- A m│
│ │<img src="green-do.gif"><a href="metadome.html"><b>Metadome</b></a>- A col│
│ │<img src="green-do.gif"><a href="assoc.html"><b>Sports Associations</b></a>-│
│ │<img src="green-do.gif"><a href="support.html"><b>Technical Support</b></a>-│
│ │<img src="green-do.gif"><a href="personal.html"><b>Employee Home Pages</b>·│
│ │<img src="green-do.gif"><a href="profile.html"><b>Company Info</b></a>- Comp·│
│ │<hr size=4><br>                                          │ ││
│ │<img align=left hspace=20 src="imslogo.gif">Whatever Your Game, ESPN's Your │
│ │<h2>Up-to-date Sports News and More</h2><a href="http://ESPNET.SportsZone│
│ │<a href="flyfish.html">COMING SOON! </a>FlyFishing lessons from some Master /│
│ │<a href="comments.html">Register to win a FREE CD-ROM</a> - We are trying to│
│ │Check out our <a href="catlog.html">catalog of Sports Instruction CD-ROM's</a>│
│ └─────────────────────────────────────────────────────────┘▼│
│ ◄                                                          ► │
│                        ┌──────┐                             │
│                        │  OK  │                             │
│                        └──────┘                             │
└─────────────────────────────────────────────────────────────┘
```

Figure 2-9. Intellimedia Sports home page in text form

sion with the HTML tags. Recall that these tags are interpreted by the browser to format the page by generating the styles and sizes of text, provide links to other documents, and retrieve image, audio, and video files. By studying these saved Web pages, you can learn a great deal that will help you when you develop your own Web page. Figure 2-9 shows the Intellimedia Sports home page in text form. You can pick out the HTML tags since they are all enclosed in *less than* (<) and *greater than* (>) signs. For example, the title of the home page, Intellimedia Sports, Inc., is surrounded by the HTML title tags (<title> and </title>). These tags and their usage are discussed in detail in Chapter 4.

You may also choose to print the current Web page. If so, the page is printed exactly as it is displayed on the screen, including all graphics. This "What You See Is What You Get" (WYSIWYG) printing capability of Web browsers is an important feature that allows users to obtain printed versions of Web pages. Figure 2-10 shows the printed version of the Intellimedia Sports home page. Note that it looks very much like the Intellimedia Sports home page displayed in Figure 2-4. In fact, the only differences are that not all of the printed Web page can be displayed on the screen and that, unless you are using a color printer, the page will be printed in black and white.

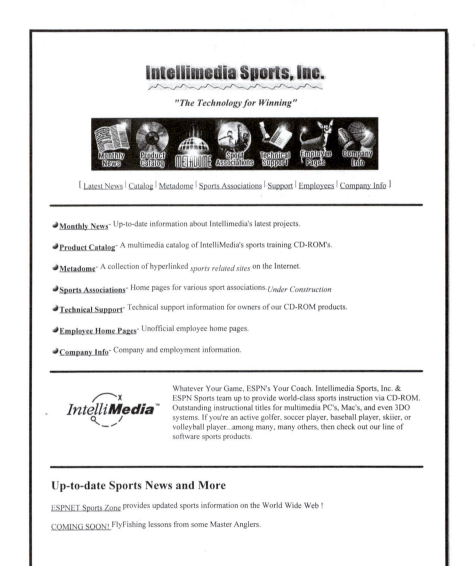

Figure 2-10. Printed version of a Web page

Forms, click-able maps, and e-mail

Three very useful features of Web pages are forms, maps, and e-mail. E-mail and forms allow you to distribute information from your Web page while maps enable you to select a Web page to visit from a graphical map.

Forms are a way for the Web page developer to accumulate information from those users who visit their Web page. When a form appears on the screen, the user simply fills it out and clicks on "Send." This automatically returns the form to the Web site where the information is interpreted. This is a great way for retailers to enable customers to order goods and services over the Web. The only problem is protecting sensitive information like credit card numbers from being stolen while the form is making its way back to the Web server; however, there are now **secure servers** that provide this protection. Security is discussed in more detail in Chapter 5. Figure 2-11 shows a form used for ordering items from another of the companies discussed in Chapter 1—Jimmy Buffett's Margaritaville Store in Key West, Florida.

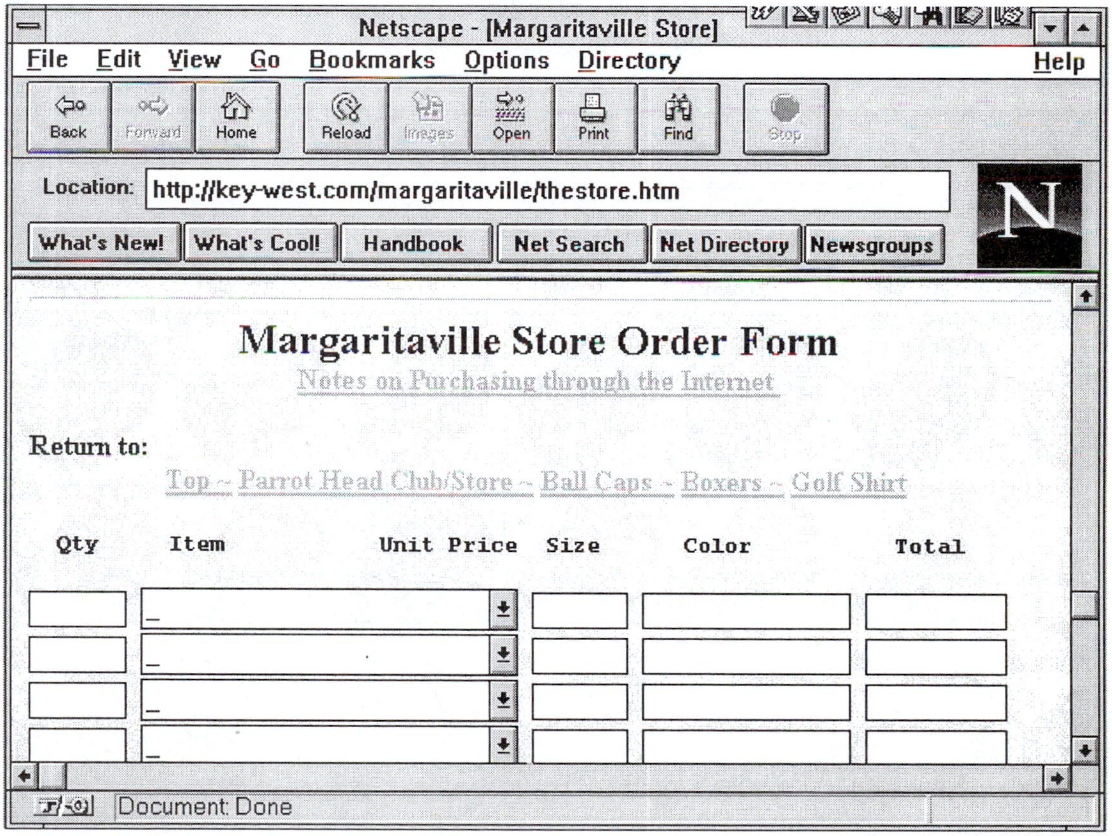

Figure 2-11. Use of forms

A **clickable map** is a graphical image on which regions act as hypertext links to other Web pages. Instead of clicking on a highlighted word or phrase to retrieve a Web pages, you click on a region of the map. Figure 2-12 shows a clickable map from the Margaritaville Store home page. In this example, the clickable map is in the form of a menu bar from which you can access any of the five options by clicking on the appropriate area.

Figure 2-12. Clickable map

You can currently send but not receive e-mail over the Web, but expect changes with future Web browsers. This process is very easy, requiring only that you select the mail option from a menu or use the mailto protocol and then fill in the recipient's name and e-mail address and the text of the message. Figure 2-13 shows how people visiting the Margaritaville's page can send messages to the page's creators by clicking on MARGARITAVILLE. All three of these operations: e-mail, forms, and clickable maps depend on Internet access and a server computer to interpret the results, so they cannot be used in a local mode

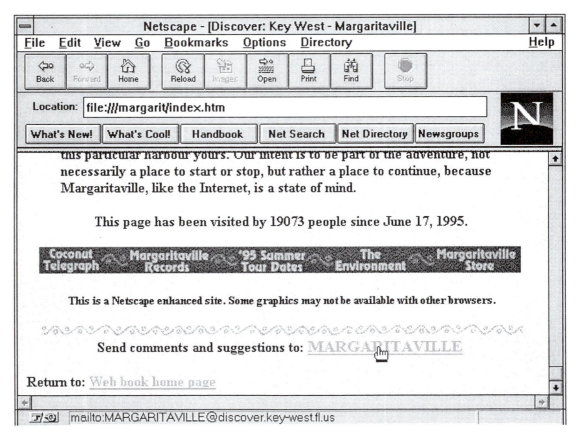

Figure 2-13. Use of return e-mail

Introduction to Netscape

As we mentioned earlier, Netscape is the most popular browser in use today. In some surveys, up to 75 percent of all persons on the Web use the Netscape browser. In this section, we will introduce you to Netscape by showing you how to access it, retrieve a home page from disk, and then move back and forth to other related Web pages. In Chapter 3, we will provide a detailed discussion of Netscape.

Accessing Netscape

Since we assume you are using Windows 3.1 to access the Netscape browser, you must first double-click on the program group icon for the group that contains Netscape. This program group typically will be named Netscape, but check with your instructor to be sure. Whatever it is, double click on the appropriate group icon. Next, you should double-click on the Netscape icon, which is a square with a capital N on a background showing the curvature of the earth. Figure 2-14 shows the Windows icon for Netscape 1.1. Other versions of Netscape will show variations of this icon. (If you are using a Macintosh, then double-click on the Netscape icon to launch the application.)

Figure 2-14. The Netscape icon in Windows 3.1

Netscape screen

After you have accessed Netscape, the Netscape screen appears. The format of this screen is the same regardless of whether you are using Windows 3.1 or 3.11 or the Macintosh, so these instructions will be the same regardless of the system. The contents of the screen, however, will differ depending on how your network manager or instructor has configured your system. The screen may come up blank or it may contain a home page that is automatically loaded when Netscape is accessed. This "home" location might be the Netscape corporate home page or some other Web site if your system is connected to the Internet and has sufficient bandwidth. On the other hand, we have created a "home" site with information on this textbook that is stored on your hard disk under the URL

file:///c:\weblearn\webbook.htm

This local file "home" site is shown in Figure 2-15.

Note in Figure 2-15 that the URL for this home page is shown in the location box. Observe that there are a series of menu options at the top of the screen beginning with File and ending with Help on the far right. There are also two rows of buttons above and below a text box in which the address of the current Web site is displayed. In this chapter, we will have you click on a link to retrieve another Web page that is stored on your disk.

Figure 2-15. "Home" Netscape page

Your turn!

1. If you are not already in Windows (or the Macintosh operating system), access it as directed by your instructor.

2. Double-click on the icon for the group that contains Netscape. (Check with your instructor about the exact group.)

3. Double-click on the Netscape icon to access the Netscape screen. The home page shown in Figure 2-15 should be displayed.

4. Point out the browser elements, that is, menu bar, buttons, Web page address, main screen, hypertext links, and graphics, on the Netscape screen.

Using a hypertext link to retrieve a web page

As an example of using a hypertext link in Netscape to retrieve a Web page, we will use the home page for this textbook shown in Figure 2-15, which has links to the Web pages for the four companies we discussed in Chapter 1—Intellimedia Sports, Albertos, Rhebokskloof Winery, and the Margaritaville Store. In this case, we will retrieve the Intellimedia Sports home page shown earlier by clicking on that link in the textbook home page. When this is done, the Intellimedia Sports home page shown in Figure 2-4 is displayed in Netscape.

Your turn!

1. Place the pointer over an underlined link to the Intellimedia Sports home page. Note that the pointer changes to a pointing finger. Notice also that the URL for the Intellimedia Sports home page (file:/// c:\weblearn\IMS\index.htm) is shown in the bottom line of the Netscape browser.

2. Single-click on the underlined link to the Intellimedia Sports home page. You should see the same Web page shown earlier as Figure 2-4.

Navigating to other web pages

In looking at the Intellimedia Sports home page on your screen, you will note that there are a new set of links to Web pages that are associated with this page. If you click on any of the graphics with blue borders or underlined words or phrases, a related Web page will be retrieved and displayed. For example, if you click on Catalog, the Web page shown in Figure 2-16 will be displayed.

You may go back to the home page by clicking on the Back button. You may then return to the Catalog page by clicking on the Forward button.

If, at any time, the process of retrieving a Web page seems to be delayed as evidenced by no action on the screen or by only a partial retrieval, you may stop the retrieval process by clicking on the Stop button or by pressing the Escape (Esc) key.

Your turn!

1. Click on the Catalog link in the Intellimedia Sports home page to retrieve the Catalog page. It should look like Figure 2-16.

2. Click on Back to return to the home page. Click on Forward to return to the Catalog Web page.

3. Return to the home page and then retrieve the Latest News Web page. Now click on Home to return to the Web book home page.

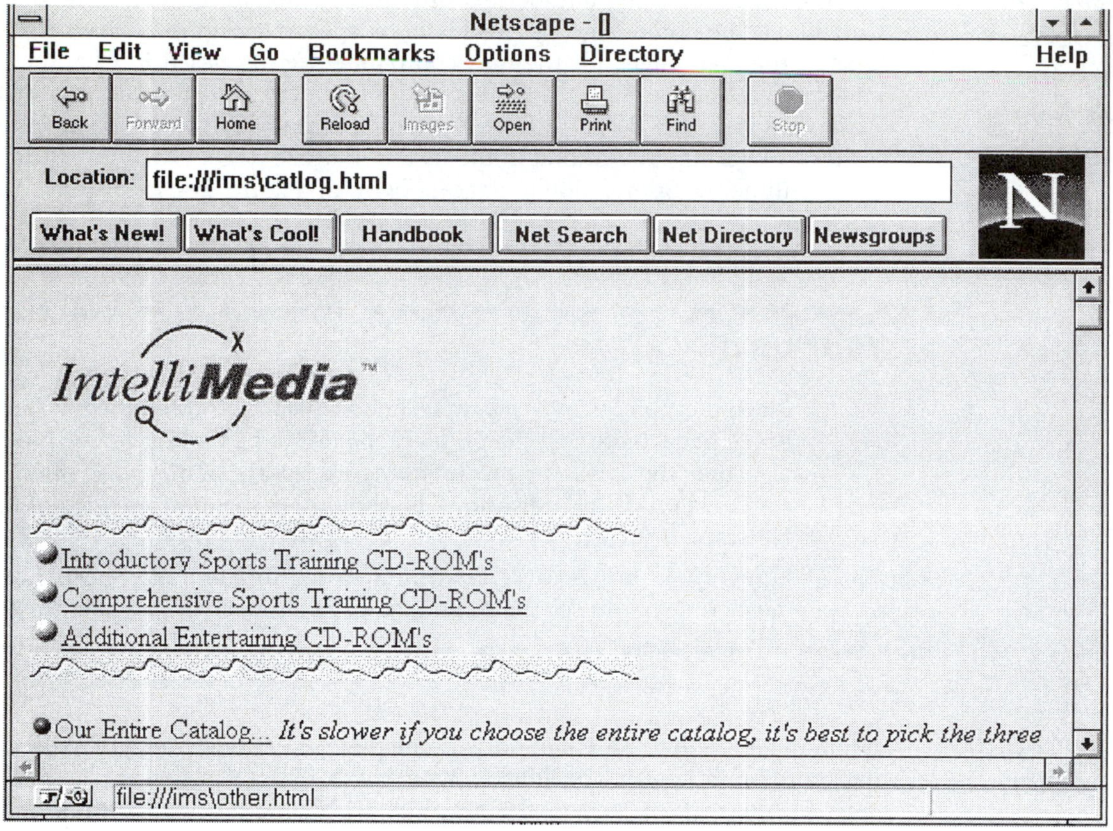

Figure 2-16. Intellimedia Sports catalog Web page

Exiting Netscape

Now that you have had a quick tour of Netscape, you can exit the browser by clicking on File and the clicking on the Exit option from the resulting pull-down menu. You may also exit Netscape by double-clicking on the Control Menu box.

- -

Your turn!

1. Exit Netscape by selecting the File option and then the Exit option.

- -

Key terms and concepts

bandwidth
browser
clickable map
client/server network
default HTML file
directory button
e-mail
file protocol
form
FTP (File Transfer Protocol)
Gopher
graphic element
helper software
home page
http (Hypertext Transfer Protocol)
hypermedia
hypertext
hypertext link
hypertext markup language (HTML)
local file

main screen
menu bar
multimedia
path
port number
protocol
scroll bars
search engine
secure server
service component
server address
Telnet
text (ascii) file
toolbar button
URL (Uniform Resource Locator)
USENET newsgroups (News)
Web page address
Web site
Web page

Exercises

1. What are the key elements of a Web browser? What is *hypermedia?*

2. What difficulties in using the Internet are discussed in the text? How do Web browsers resolve these problems?

3. What are five primary Internet applications in addition to the Web?

4. What was the nature of the first Web browsers? How do current browsers differ from the original browsers?

5. What is a Web page? What is a home page? Are all Web pages also home pages? Why or why not?

6. What are the primary elements of a browser? What is a *clickable link?*

7. List and briefly discuss each of the key browser operations. Describe the reformatting operation.

8. What are the parts of a URL? List five protocols and their purpose. What is the purpose of a default HTML file?

9. Why do we ask you to retrieve local files rather than retrieving them from the Internet? What does bandwidth have to do with this?

10. Why are helper software packages needed?

11. What are Bookmarks? What browser operation do they facilitate? What is a search engine?

12. What are forms used for? How are they related to business use of the Web? Why are secure servers needed?

13. Access Netscape using Windows 3.1 or 3.11 (or the Macintosh). From the "home" Web page that appears when you access Netscape, click on <u>Margaritaville</u> to view Jimmy Buffett's Margaritaville Store home page. Click on Back to return to the Web book home page.

14. Click on <u>Alberto's</u> to view Alberto's Nightclub home page. Click on Back to return to the Web book home page.

15. Click on <u>Rhebok</u> to view the home page for the Rhebokskloof Winery in South Africa. Click on File from the menu bar, then click on Exit to exit Netscape.

3   Using Netscape

■ ■

Objectives

After completing this chapter, you will be able to:

❖ discuss the use of the Netscape browser to navigate the Web;

❖ access Netscape and describe the various parts of Netscape;

❖ use the Netscape toolbar buttons to carry out browser operations;

❖ use the menu bar to carry out the same operations as the toolbar in addition to handling other important operations;

❖ control the appearance of the Netscape screen and change various default settings;

❖ discuss the use of the Directory buttons to carry out a variety of operations.

Introduction

As with other Web browsers, the primary purpose of Netscape is to access the ever growing number of Web pages. In this chapter, we will briefly review accessing Netscape and then discuss its parts. We will then discuss in detail how to use Netscape to perform the key browser operations listed in Chapter 2. We will also discuss other operations that can be accomplished with Netscape. Throughout this discussion, you will note that there are usually two or more ways to carry out most operations. You can use a menu option to perform an operation or use one of the two sets of buttons located beneath the menu bar to do the same thing. For example, there are three ways to enter the URL of a Web page: use a button, use a menu option, or enter the URL directly in the location box. As you become familiar with Netscape, you may find that you favor one method over another. You should use the most comfortable one.

Accessing Netscape

If you are using Windows 3.1, you must first double-click on the group that contains the Netscape icon to access Netscape. Next, double-click on the Netscape icon which is a square with a capital N on a background of the Earth's silhouette. After you double-click on the Netscape icon, the opening home page is displayed (Figure 3-1). Recall that the **opening home page** is a Web page loaded when you access Netscape. In this case, the opening home page contains information about this textbook plus links to other Web pages.

Figure 3-1. Opening home page

Using local files

As we discussed in Chapter 2, your instructor has been provided with a disk on which a variety of Web page files have been stored. To avoid the problems that can be encountered when a group of students all try to access the same Web site on the Internet, we will ask that you access these local Web pages. The process of accessing a local home page and one on the Web is exactly the same with one exception: a different URL. The URL for a Web page is composed of **http://** plus the Web server name and the path name of the Web page.

On the other hand, the URL for a local file is composed of **file:///** plus the path of the Web page file (including the drive letter). For example, the URL for the Intellimedia Sports, Inc. home page on the Internet is:

http://www.intellimedia.com/index.html

The URL for the same home page stored on disk is:

file:///c:\weblearn\ims\index.htm

Note that the local URL path name uses backslashes (\) because we are working on a Windows system (in the case of a Macintosh, use a forward slash (/)). When we ask you to access a local Web page, we will give you the local URL; however, in case you have access to the Web and your instructor permits it, see the Web URL in Table 2-4.

■ ■

Your turn!

1. Access Netscape from your PC.
2. What is the URL of the starting home page that loads automatically when you access Netscape?
3. Why do we suggest you access local files when using this book?

■ ■

Elements of the Netscape window

Once you have accessed Netscape, the screen will look nearly the same regardless of whether you are using Windows 3.1, Windows 3.11, Macintosh, or X-Windows. The same Web Book home page shown in Figure 3-1 is shown again in Figure 3-2 with the various elements indicated. The elements on the Netscape screen are shown in Table 3-1, with a short description of each.

Table 3-1: Summary of Netscape screen elements

Netscape element	Description
Title bar	The title of the Web page
Menu bar	The main menu options
Toolbar	Buttons which activate important Netscape commands
Location window	The address of the current Web page
Status indicator	Netscape's corporate logo; animated when a page is being retrieved
Directory buttons	Buttons which provide access to interesting or useful Web pages
Content area	The contents of the Web page
Security indicator	The security status of the Web page
Progress bar	The status of the retrieval; also displays the URL of a hypertext link

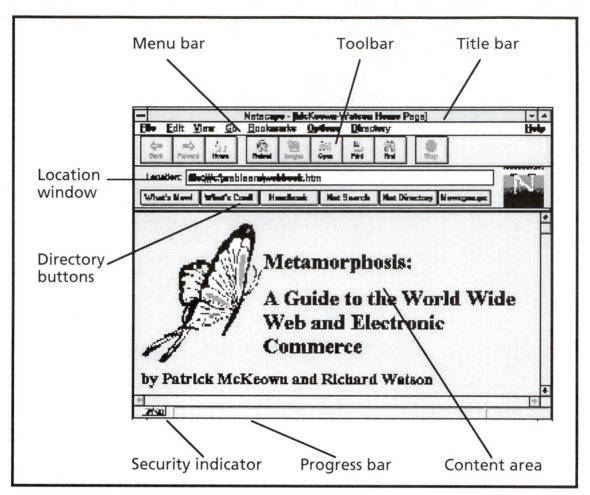

Figure 3-2. Elements of the Netscape screen

We will discuss the function of each of the elements of Netscape. You do not need to learn how to use all of them since, in many cases, they provide different ways of doing the same thing. In fact, Netscape gives you the option to remove some of them from the screen if you find them unnecessary. (However, do not modify the Netscape screen in a computer lab environment without first checking with your instructor.)

Title bar

The **title bar** displays the title of the home page you have retrieved. In this case, the title bar shows that the home page is titled "McKeown-Watson Home Page." If no page has been loaded, the title page shows "Netscape."

Menu bar

The **menu bar** of the Netscape screen provides you with a variety of options from which to choose. These include: File, Edit, View, Go, Bookmarks, Options, Directory, and Help. Corresponding to each menu bar option is a submenu with specific commands. For example, the submenu of the File menu option has eleven commands, including accessing, printing, and saving a Web page. In fact, *all* of the commands necessary to navigate the Web with Netscape are available via the menu bar options.

Toolbar

Located beneath the menu bar, the **toolbar** consists of nine command buttons. While all of these commands are available via the menu bar, they are more accessible from these clickable buttons. For example, the File submenu options of Open and Print a home page are also available as toolbar buttons, as is the option to return to the opening home page (Home).

Location window

The **location window** is located immediately beneath the toolbar. The URL of the page currently displayed on the screen is shown in the location window. For example, for the Web Book home page shown in Figure 3-2, the location window contains the URL of the local Web Book home page, that is, file:/// c:\weblearn\webbook.htm.

Status indicator

To the right of the location window is the **status indicator,** which is in the form of the Netscape corporate logo. The logo's form depends on the version of Netscape you use. For example, for Version 1.1, it is a large N superimposed on the Earth's curvature. When you request that a Web page is loaded, the status indicator will animate in some way. In many cases, the text will load rather quickly, but the images may take a few minutes to load and the status indicator will continue to be active. As noted in Chapter 2, a useful feature of Netscape is that you may read the text while images are loading.

Directory buttons

The **directory buttons** located directly beneath the location window correspond to a special set of home pages that Netscape developers believe to be useful to users. These buttons include What's New!, What's Cool!, Handbook, Net Search, Net Directory, and Newsgroups. Clicking on any of these buttons links you to a home page with more information on that particular topic. The directory buttons will be discussed in detail in Chapter 5.

Content area

The **content area** of the Netscape window is where the actual HTML-formatted text and inline images of the current page are displayed. Horizontal and vertical scroll bars will allow you to view parts of a page that is larger than the screen. The text in this content area can be selected and copied to another Windows document or it can be saved or printed. There also may be icons in the content area that correspond to large images, audio, or video files. When one of these icons is clicked, the helper software discussed in Chapter 2 will display the image or play the file.

Security area

In the bottom left-hand corner of the Netscape window is the **security area,** which displays a door key. If the door key is displayed on a blue background, then the home page is considered secure--that is, it is not susceptible to fraud and other misuse by hackers or other electronic criminals. This is an extremely important issue for companies that are interested in doing business on the Web. They must be able to send and receive information over the Internet with the knowledge that no one can eavesdrop on the message, copy it, or otherwise damage the contents. A secure Web page means that users can send credit card numbers over the Web without having to worry about it being intercepted by a hacker. If the door key is shown on a grey background, then the home page is insecure and there is no guarantee that information will not be stolen, copied, or damaged. Security will be discussed in more detail in Chapter 5.

Progress bar

At the very bottom of the Netscape window is the **progress bar** that uses both text and graphics to display the status of loading a Web page as well as other useful information. In the bottom right-hand corner is the graphic progress indicator which is a red bar showing how much of a Web page has been loaded. When loading is complete, the graphic progress bar disappears.

In the bottom center, the text progress bar provides a variety of information. When a the Netscape pointer is positioned over a hypertext link, the progress bar displays the corresponding URL. The text progress bar will also show the URL of each file that is being loaded and then display the status of the loading process in terms of bytes of information loaded relative to the total number of bytes in the file. When the process is completed, the progress bar will display the message "Document: Done."

■ ■

Your turn!

1. Once the opening Web Book home page is on screen, point out the parts of the Netscape window. If this page is not on the screen, position the mouse pointer over the Home toolbar button and click the left mouse button *once.*

2. Position the mouse pointer over the Open toolbar button and click the left mouse button *once.* Press the Escape (Esc) key to cancel this operation.

3. Position the pointer on the Intellimedia Sports, Inc. link and note the URL of this Web page in the progress bar. Do the same for the Rhebokskloof home page.

■ ■

Working with Web pages

Now that you know the elements of the Netscape window, you are ready to use Netscape to navigate the Web. In this chapter, we will discuss using Netscape to carry out several operations on the Web, including:

❖ retrieving a home page;

❖ linking to other Web pages;

❖ navigating among Web pages;

❖ retrieving previously viewed Web pages;

❖ saving and printing Web pages;

Other Netscape operations will be covered in subsequent chapters.

Point and click navigation

One of the valuable features of Netscape and other graphical browsers is **point and click navigation**, in which you use your mouse or other pointing device to position the pointer over a hypertext link, the menu bar, tool bar, location window, or directory buttons. You can then click a mouse button to execute the corresponding command.

The Netscape pointer changes shape depending on where it is positioned. Usually, the pointer is an arrow and, if the pointer is positioned over a menu item or button and the left mouse button clicked, the corresponding menu item or button will be selected. If the pointer is positioned over the location window, the pointer changes to a vertical line, which allows you to delete an existing URL and enter a new one into the location window. Finally, when positioned over a hypertext link, the pointer changes to a hand with pointing finger. If you click the left mouse button, the corresponding Web page will be retrieved. Figure 3-3 shows the pointer positioned over a hypertext link. Note that the arrow has changed to a pointing finger. Note also that the URL of the corresponding Web page is displayed in the progress bar.

It is important to note that in *all* cases involving a selection with the Netscape pointer, you only need to click the left mouse button *once*, not twice as with many Windows operations.

- -

Your turn!

1. Move the pointer to the Alberto's Nightclub link on the Web Book home page and click the left mouse button to retrieve this page.

2. Move the pointer to the location window and click the left mouse button. Delete the existing URL.

3. Enter the URL for the Web Book home page:

   file:///c:\weblearn\webbook.htm

   and press Enter. You should now be back at the Web Book home page.

- -

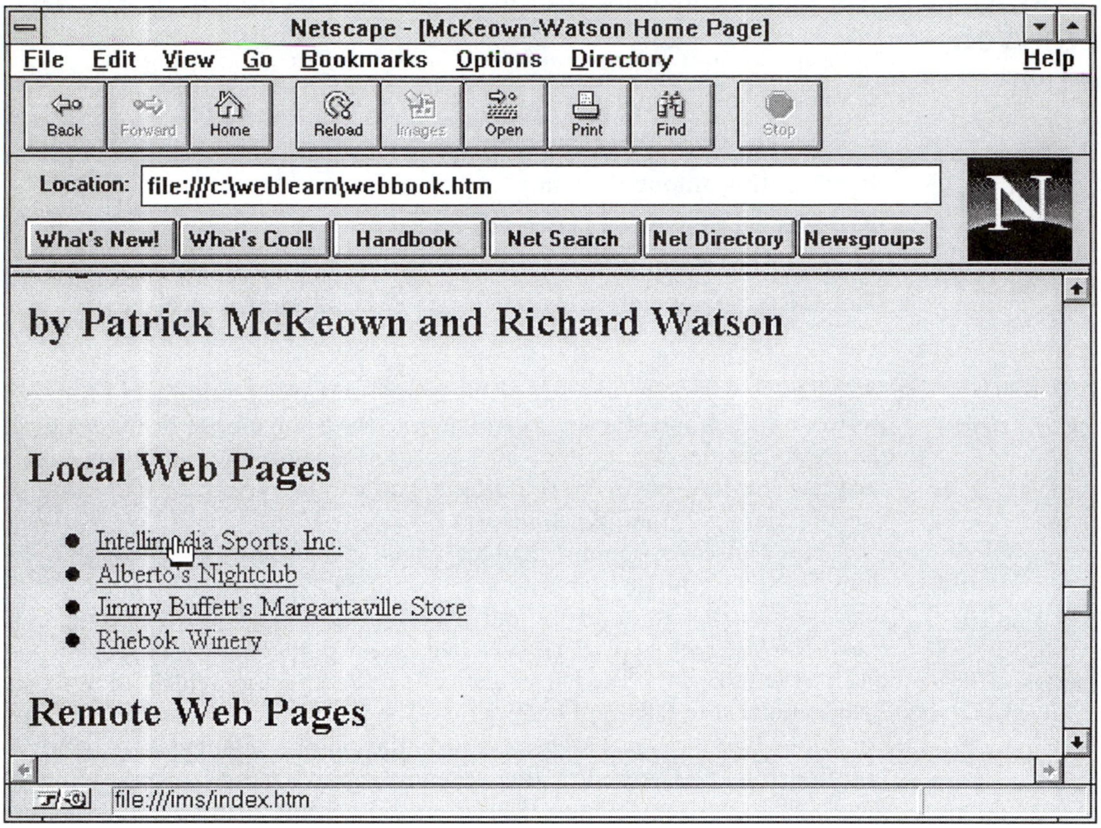

Netscape - [McKeown-Watson Home Page]

File   Edit   View   Go   Bookmarks   Options   Directory   Help

Back   Forward   Home   Reload   Images   Open   Print   Find   Stop

Location: file:///c:\weblearn\webbook.htm   N

What's New!   What's Cool!   Handbook   Net Search   Net Directory   Newsgroups

by Patrick McKeown and Richard Watson

Local Web Pages

- Intellimedia Sports, Inc.
- Alberto's Nightclub
- Jimmy Buffett's Margaritaville Store
- Rhebok Winery

Remote Web Pages

file:///ims/index.htm

Figure 3-3. Hypertext pointer

Using the toolbar

The easiest way to navigate the Web and work with Web pages is to use the toolbar. Recall that the toolbar is located immediately beneath the menu bar and contains nine buttons. To use a toolbar button, simply position the pointer over the button and click the mouse button. Figure 3-4 shows the Netscape toolbar.

Figure 3-4. Netscape toolbar

The nine buttons on the toolbar are divided into three groups: navigation, file operations, and stop. The navigation buttons allow you to move around previously retrieved home pages while the file operations buttons carry out various operations with the Web page files, including opening and printing them. The Stop button cancels the loading process whenever the process is taking too long or you decide not to complete retrieval. As an example of a file operation to retrieve a Web page, you would simply click on the Open button to display the Open Location dialog box as shown in Figure 3-5 and enter the URL for the desired Web page.

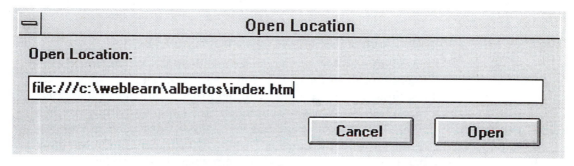

Figure 3-5. The open location dialog box

When a remote Web page is retrieved through either a hypertext link or by entering a URL in the location box or in the Open Location dialog box, the browser goes through four steps:

looking for the server with the address shown in this URL;

connecting to the server;

waiting for a reply;

transferring the Web page file to the user's machine.

During this process, the progress bar at the bottom of the screen shows the status of the retrieval. Note that when a local Web page is retrieved, the page is retrieved from a hard disk and displayed on the screen without going through the first three steps.

To navigate among Web pages, you can use the Back and Forward toolbar buttons. The Back button returns you to a previously viewed Web page and the Forward button goes *forward* through a series of previously viewed Web pages. The Home button automatically retrieves the opening home page. The location of this Web page is usually defined by the person installing Netscape and can be a local page or a page somewhere on the Internet.

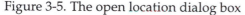

Your turn!

1. With the Web Book home page displayed, click on the Intellimedia Sports hypertext link. Now, click on the Open button and enter the following URL:

   file:///c:\weblearn\albertos\index.htm

   to retrieve the local Web page for Alberto's Night Club.

2. Click on the Back button to return to the previous (Intellimedia) page.

3. Click on the Forward button to return to Alberto's home page.

4. Click on the Home button to return to the Web Book home page that was originally loaded when you accessed Netscape.

Small companies hope to take advantage of Internet

Based on a Gallup survey of 300 attendees at a White House Conference on Small Business in June 1995, many small business owners think that the Internet will help them compete in the global marketplace. While most of them ran companies with fewer than 10 employees, 57 percent said the Internet offered as many opportunities for them as for the Fortune 500 companies. On the other hand, 30 percent expressed concern about finding relevant information on the Internet. In response, MCI is adding a Small Business Center to its World Wide Web site.

In another survey, MCI found specific areas in which small businesses are taking advantage of the Internet. In this study, 68 percent of the respondents said that they found the Internet useful for keeping up with current trends and 65 percent said that they used it to research information. Also, 60 percent said that they used the Internet to purchase products and services and to use e-mail to make contacts with customers, suppliers, and colleagues. Finally, over 50 percent said they hoped to use the Internet to reach new customers. The results of this study are shown graphically below.

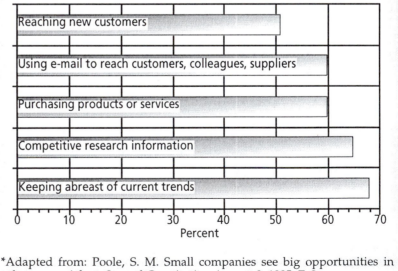

*Adapted from: Poole, S. M. Small companies see big opportunities in cyberspace. *Atlanta Journal-Constitution*. August 9, 1995. F: 2

Other tool-bar buttons

In addition to the Open button and the three navigation buttons, there are five other buttons. To print the currently displayed Web page, you can use the Print button. This will display the Windows Print dialog window in which you can click OK to activate printing or click Cancel to cancel the process.

To search for a word or phrase in the current Web page, you can click on the Find button. This will display the Find dialog box in which you enter the word or phrase. This is *not* the same as searching for a Web page on a particular topic. It is like the "find" operation available in word processing software. For example, to search for the word "CD-ROM" in the Intellimedia Sports home page, you would click on the Find button and then fill in the dialog box. When this is done, the word or phrase is highlighted in the Web page. The Reload toolbar button is used to request that a Web page be retrieved. The Reload process is necessary if the Web page is somehow corrupted during Internet transmission. Graphics may be only partially displayed or text can be "garbage" or conflict with images. If this occurs, then clicking on Reload automatically retrieves the current Web page.

It is possible to set up Netscape so only the text of a Web page will be retrieved without images. This may be done if the Web page is being retrieved over a modem or if the connection to the server is slow due to heavy traffic. If you then decide that you wish to view the missing images, click on the Images toolbar button. Figure 3-6 and Figure 3-7 show content area of the Intellimedia Sports' home page without images and after the Image button is clicked.

Netscape keeps both a memory cache and a disk cache. A **memory cache** is a copy of recent Web pages in computer memory and a **disk cache** is a larger number of recently visited Web pages stored on disk. Thus, recently visited Web pages can be retrieved more quickly from memory or disk than from a distant Web site.

Finally, the Stop button terminates the retrieval process. Slow retrieval of a Web page is seldom a problem when retrieving local Web page files, but it can be a major issue when retrieving a remote Web page that contains many images, or very large images over the Internet. This is especially true when you are retrieving Web pages over a modem.

Your turn!

1. Use the toolbar's Home button to retrieve the Web Book home page and then use the toolbar Print button to print it (check with your instructor before beginning this process).

2. Click on the toolbar's Find button, enter the word "Web," and press Enter. You should now see the word "Web" highlighted in the Web Book home page. Press Esc to cancel the Find process.

3. Click on the toolbar's Reload Button to retrieve the Web Book home page again.

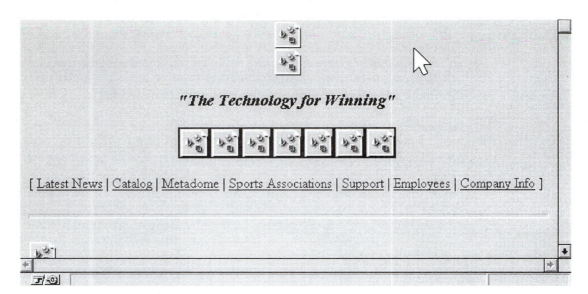

Figure 3-6. A Web page without images

Figure 3-7. A Web page with images

Summary of toolbar buttons

Table 3-2 displays the nine toolbar buttons along with their groups and purpose. We have also shown the shortcut key combinations that can be used instead of clicking a button. **Shortcut keys** often use the Ctrl key in conjunction with a letter. For example, you can select the Open option directly by pressing Ctrl-L instead of clicking on the toolbar Open button.

Table 3-2: Toolbar buttons

Button	Group	Purpose	Shortcut Key
Back	Navigation	Move backward to a previous page	Ctrl + Left Arrow
Forward	Navigation	Move forward to a previous page	Ctrl + Right Arrow
Home	Navigation	Move to the page that is retrieved when Netscape is accessed	None
Reload	File operation	Start the retrieval process again (used when a page is corrupted during display)	Ctrl + R
Images	File operation	Load images if they were not loaded with the text	Ctrl + I
Open	File operation	Display Open Location dialog box for entry of a URL	Ctrl + L
Print	File operation	Print the currently displayed page	None
Find	File operation	Look for a word or phrase in the *currently* displayed page (does *not* search for home pages)	Ctrl + F
Stop	Stop	Terminate the retrieval of a page (used if the transfer process is too slow)	Esc (Escape)

About the menu bar

So far, we have covered the use of the mouse pointer and toolbar buttons to handle two of the browser operations listed earlier (retrieving a Web page and linking to other Web pages) and parts of two other operations (navigating among Web pages and printing a Web page). To accomplish the remaining browser operations, you must use the menu bar. As discussed previously, *all* of the necessary commands in Netscape can be accomplished by the eight menu bar options: File, Edit, View, Go, Bookmarks, Options, Directory, and Help. This includes the toolbar button operations just discussed. Each of these menu bar options has a submenu from which you then select the actual command. The menu bar is shown in Figure 3-8.

Netscape - [Web Book Home Page]

<u>F</u>ile   <u>E</u>dit   <u>V</u>iew   <u>G</u>o   <u>B</u>ookmarks   <u>O</u>ptions   <u>D</u>irectory   <u>H</u>elp

Figure 3-8. Netscape menu bar

You may select an option from the menu bar in a variety of ways:

❖ by pressing Alt to highlight the menu bar options and then using the left and right arrow keys to move the highlighting to the desired option;

❖ by pressing simultaneously Alt and the first letter of the desired option;

❖ by positioning the mouse pointer over the desired option and clicking the left mouse button once.

For example, to select the File option from the menu bar, you could press Alt and then use the right arrow key to move the highlighting to File and press Enter. Since the F in File is underlined, you could also press Alt-F (that is press and hold down the Alt key and press the F key) to access the File menu option. Finally, you could position the mouse pointer (an arrow) over the File option and single-click the left mouse button. Once the menu bar File option has been selected, a submenu appears (see Figure 3-9). In any case, you can cancel the option selection by either pressing the Esc (Escape) key or by moving the mouse pointer off the submenu and clicking the left mouse button.

New Window	Ctrl+N
Open Location...	Ctrl+L
Open File...	Ctrl+O
Save as...	Ctrl+S
Mail Document...	Ctrl+M
Document Info	
Print...	
Print Preview	
Close	Ctrl+W
Exit	

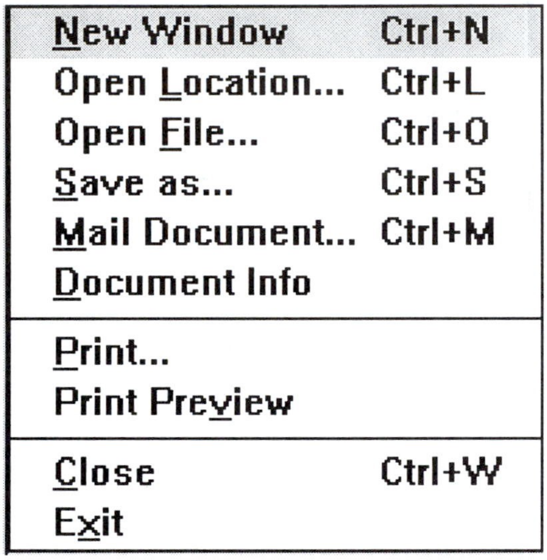

Figure 3-9. The File submenu

Your turn!

1. Access the menu bar using the Alt key and then highlight the File option. Compare the drop down menu you see with Figure 3-9. Press the Escape (Esc) key to cancel this operation.

2. Access the File option on the menu bar directly by using the Alt key plus F. You should see the same drop down menu as in the previous exercise. Press Esc to cancel this operation.

3. Access the File option on the menu bar by using your mouse or other pointing device. Press Esc to cancel this operation.

Executing menu commands

Once you have a drop down submenu for a menu bar option, you can select from it using one of three methods:

❖ use the up and down arrow keys to move the highlighting to the command and press Enter;

❖ position the pointer over the command and click the left mouse button;

❖ press the underlined letter of the option.

If you choose to use the last method, you should be aware that while the first letter of the submenu option is often the underlined letter, this is not always the case. Note also that you do NOT need to press the Alt key before pressing a letter to make a selection from a submenu. For example, if you selected the File menu option as discussed previously, you can then select the Open Location option by pressing L, since the L in Location is underlined.

Figure 3-9 shows the shortcut keys for many of the File submenu selections. This is true for each of the first five menu options, and you can use a shortcut key to bypass the menu bar and submenus.

Your turn!

1. Access the File option from the menu bar and highlight Open Location to select this command from the drop down menu. Press Esc to cancel this operation.

2. Access the File option from the menu bar and press L to select the Open Location command from the drop down menu. Press Esc to cancel this operation.

3. Without going to the menu bar, use the Ctrl + L shortcut key to display the Open Location dialog box. Press Esc to cancel this operation.

4. Use two ways to access the Find command (Ctrl + A) from the Edit option on the menu bar. In both cases, press Esc to cancel this operation.

Overview of menu options

There are eight options on the menu bar that Table 3-3 summarizes. Note that the first six options involve actual commands that affect the operation of Netscape, while the last two retrieve home pages to your screen, which provide you with interesting information or help in using Netscape. Since the home pages listed in the Directory and Help submenus require access to the Web over the Internet, we suggest that you *not* select any of these home pages unless told to do so.

Table 3-3: Menu option command summary

Menu option	Command summary
File	Opens or closes URLs or local files, saves or prints home pages, sends e-mail, or exits Netscape
Edit	Enables copying of portions of home pages or finding words or phrases in a home page
View	Controls loading of home pages and images
Go	Enables navigation between home pages and shows history of the current Netscape session
Bookmarks	Lists previously saved URLs of home pages and enables saving the current URL
Options	Controls the appearance of the Netscape screen and other settings
Directory	Lists interesting and useful home pages
Help	Provides a variety of help tools including an on-line handbook and reference source

Your turn!

1. Select the View menu bar option and note the commands listed in the drop down menu.

2. Select the Options menu bar option and note which of the commands are checked. If the Show Toolbar command is checked, click on it. What happens to the Netscape screen? Now click on the Options button again and note the result.

3. Access the Help menu bar option and then select *About Netscape*. This tells you which version of Netscape you are using.

Using the menu bar options

In this section, we will discuss each of these eight options and the corresponding submenus in some detail. In several instances, the commands in the submenus have already been discussed in the section on the toolbar buttons.

Using the File submenu

As shown in Figure 3-9, the File submenu has ten options, the most of any submenu. The Open Location... and Print... submenu options are the same as the toolbar Open and Print buttons. In this section, we will discuss the remaining File submenu options.

To open additional Netscape windows, you would use the New Window option from the File submenu. Recall that Windows allows multiple tasks to be undertaken at the same time and this includes having multiple Netscape windows open. For example, you can have the Web Book home page open in one window and the Intellimedia Sports home page open in another window. You can resize or move the windows as needed or close a window with the Close command. Figure 3-10 shows two Netscape windows open simultaneously.

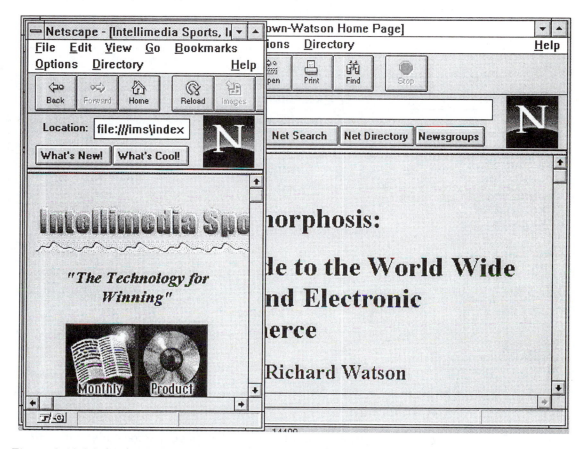

Figure 3-10. Multiple Netscape windows

If you are opening a local file Web page, you can enter the URL by using the toolbar Open button or Open Location... command. You can also use the Open File... command. If the latter approach is used, the File Open dialog box is displayed as shown in Figure 3-11.

From the Open File dialog box, you can use the list boxes to select a drive (a:, c:, and so on), select a directory, and then select a htm file. For example, if c:\weblearn has been set up as the working directory for Netscape, you should see the htm file list for this directory plus a list of directories corresponding to the four companies discussed in Chapter 1. You can double-click a directory to see the htm files in it and then single-click on a htm file and click OK to select it. Note that since you are not required to go through a home page to view an associated Web page, *all* Web pages with an extension of htm are displayed in this list.

To save a Web page to a local file with a htm extension, you can use the Save As... command. If you select this command, then the Save As... dialog box displays the default drive, directory, and file name. You can change any of these as needed. As discussed in Chapter 2, the images are *not* saved as a part of the local file that you are creating. If you retrieve a saved local file into Netscape, it will look like Figure 3-6.

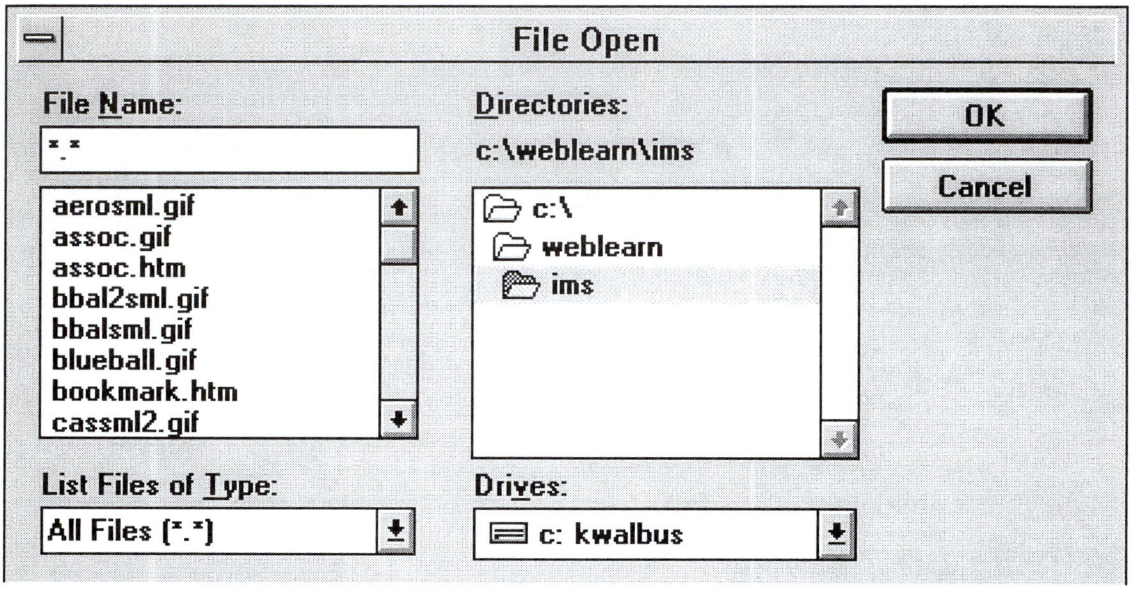

Figure 3-11. Open file dialog box

- -

A quick hint

If you wish to save the images in a Web page to a local file with a gif extension, position the pointer over the image and click the right mouse button and then select "Save this image as...." Enter the name of the file in the Save As... dialog box.

- -

As we have already mentioned, you can use the Netscape browser for *outgoing* e-mail. To do this, select the Mail Document... command from the File submenu. If this command is selected, an outgoing e-mail screen like that in Figure 3-12 is displayed. To send a message, fill in the address of the recipient and then tab down to the message area and type the message. Finally, click the Send button.

```
┌─────────────────────────────────────────────────────────────────────┐
│ ▭                      Send Mail / Post News                          │
├─────────────────────────────────────────────────────────────────────┤
│      From:  Patrick McKeown <pmckeown@uga.cc.uga.edu>                  │
│                 ┌───────────────────────────────────────────────────┐ │
│    Mail To:     │ rwatson@uga.cc.uga.edu                            │ │
│                 └───────────────────────────────────────────────────┘ │
│                 ┌───────────────────────────────────────────────────┐ │
│ Post Newsgroup: │                                                   │ │
│                 └───────────────────────────────────────────────────┘ │
│                 ┌───────────────────────────────────────────────────┐ │
│    Subject:     │ file:///c:\weblearn\webbook.htm                   │ │
│                 └───────────────────────────────────────────────────┘ │
│                 ┌─────────────────────────────────────┐  ┌──────────┐ │
│ Attachment:     │                                     │  │ Attach...│ │
│                 └─────────────────────────────────────┘  └──────────┘ │
│ ┌───────────────────────────────────────────────────────────────┐ ▲ │
│ │ Rick:                                                           │   │
│ │                                                                 │   │
│ │ What do you think about including outgoing e-mail in our book.  │   │
│ │ It seems like a very interesting topic. Let me know your        │   │
│ │ thoughts.                                                       │   │
│ │                                                                 │   │
│ │ Pat                                                             │ ▼ │
│ └───────────────────────────────────────────────────────────────┘   │
│  ┌──────────┐        ┌──────────────────┐        ┌──────────┐        │
│  │   Send   │        │  Quote Document  │        │  Cancel  │        │
│  └──────────┘        └──────────────────┘        └──────────┘        │
└─────────────────────────────────────────────────────────────────────┘
```

Figure 3-12. Netscape e-mail screen

To view information about a Web page, select the Document Info command from the File submenu. This will display a screen containing the document title, page location, date of last modification, and other information about the security status of the Web page.

To preview the Web page that will be printed if the Print button is clicked or the Print...command selected, select the Print Preview command from the File submenu. Finally, to exit Netscape, select the Exit command from the File submenu. Note: if you only have one Netscape window open, then selecting the Close command will have the same effect as the Exit command.

■ ▬ ■ ▬ ■ ▬ ■ ▬ ■ ▬ ■ ▬ ■ ▬ ■ ▬ ■ ▬ ■ ▬ ■ ▬ ■ ▬ ■ ▬

Your turn!

1. If the Web Book home page is not displayed in Netscape, click on the Home button to display it. With a formatted disk in the a: drive, use the Save as... command to save the current Web page to your disk, with a name of a:\textbook.htm.

2. Use the New Window command to open a new Netscape window. Note that the Web Book home page is displayed in this new window. Why? Now use the Open File... command to retrieve the a:\textbook.htm file into this window in Netscape. Resize this window and compare the two versions of the Web Book home page. Use the Close command to close this window.

3. Use the Document Info command to display information on the Text-book home page. When was it last modified? Now use the Print Preview command to see how the page would look if it were printed.

━ ━

Using the Edit sub-menu

The second menu option, Edit, may be the least used of the Netscape menu options. It has only five commands and only two—Copy and Find—are used. The remaining commands, Undo, Cut, and Paste, are greyed out and cannot be selected. The Copy command is used to copy highlighted text to the Windows clipboard, where it can then be pasted into another Windows application, but not into the Netscape content screen. For example, the Copy command can be used to copy information from the Netscape screen into the e-mail window. The Find command is the same as the Find button on the toolbar.

Using the View sub-menu

The View submenu has four options: Reload, Load Images, Refresh, and Source.... For our purposes, the Reload and Refresh commands are the same as the Reload button on the toolbar menu and the Load Images command is the same as the Images button. The last command, Source..., displays the HTML source code for the Web document. You can only view the source code; it cannot be created or modified with Netscape. Figure 3-13 shows the result of using the Source command for the Web Book home page.

```
View Source

<html>
<title>Intellimedia Sports, Inc.</title>
<body>
<center><img src="ims.gif"></center>
<center><img src="wavey.gif"></center>
<center><h3><i>"The Technology for Winning"</i></h3></center>
<center><a href="newprod.html><img src="newprod.gif></a><a href="catlog.html"><img src="cat
personal.html"><img src="emply.gif" ></a><a href="profile.html"><img src="cominfo.gif"</a></a>
<br>
<center>
[ <a href="newprod.html">Latest News</a> | <a href="catlog.html">Catalog</a> | <a href="metac

                                    OK
```

Figure 3-13. Using the source command

Using the Go sub-menu

The Go submenu has five commands, four of which are the same as toolbar buttons. The Back, Forward, and Home commands are the same as the toolbar buttons with the same names while the Stop Loading command is the same as the Stop button. The remaining command, View History, will display a partial list of Web sites that have been recently visited plus the current Web page with a checkmark beside it. The History list is shown below the sub-menu, and you can go directly to a site by clicking on the Web page name. You can also select the View History command to see a more complete description of these pages. You should be aware that the "history" only shows the most recently visited Web page and any Web pages that can be reached from it. For example, if you selected the Alberto's home page from the Web Book home page and then looked at the Directions page and then returned to the Web Book home page, both the Alberto's and the Directions pages would be in the history list. If you then selected the Intellimedia Sports home page, only it and the current page would be included in the history list.

Steve Jobs comments on the Web

In 1976, Steve Jobs and Steve Wozniak founded the Apple Computer Company to sell the personal computers they were building in a garage. For nine years, Jobs served in various positions with the company, including president and chairman of the board, as it grew into a giant in the personal computer field. During this time, he was instrumental in developing both the extremely popular Apple II and Macintosh lines of computers, the latter being notable for its graphical user interface and easy-to-use operating system.

In 1985, Jobs left Apple to found a new company—NeXT, Inc. Initially established to build a new workstation, NeXT now markets a software product called WebObjects, which allows programmers to build interactive Web sites rapidly. In an interview, Jobs said that people will eventually do four things on the Web: static publishing, dynamic publishing, commerce, and internal custom applications. Static publishing refers to someone creating a Web page that doesn't change unless the creator changes it. In dynamic publishing, the computer constructs the Web page based on input from users and information in a database. The Federal Express Web site is an example of a dynamic Web page. With the third type of Web page—commerce—a company links the Web to its internal computer system so that consumers can order goods and services over the Web. Finally, with an internal custom application, a company puts its own applications on the Web so that anybody in the company can use the application. Jobs feels that his company's software will help people develop the latter three types of Web applications ten times faster than by using existing programming languages.

Adapted from: Rogers, A. In Search of a Sequel. *Newsweek*. September 4, 1995: 52.

Your turn!

1. Use the Find command to search for all occurrences of Richard Watson's name in the Web Book home page.

2. Use the Source command to view the source document for the Web Book home page. It should look like Figure 3-13.

3. From the Web Book home page, go to Alberto's home page and then to the Directions page. Use the Back button twice to return to the Web Book home page and view the history list. Now select the Intellimedia Sports home page and then return to the Web Book page and view history again. How has it changed?

Using the Bookmarks submenu

Recall from Chapter 2 that we discussed saving the URLs of interesting Web pages. To save the URL of the current home page or to access the URL of previously recorded visits to home pages in Netscape, use the Bookmark option. It has only two commands: Add Bookmark and View Bookmarks, plus a list of previously saved bookmarks to home pages. You may visit any of these home pages by simply clicking on its name. You may add the current Web page to the Bookmark list by clicking on the Add Bookmark option. If this is done and you click on Bookmarks again, you will note that it has been added. You may also view a more complete bookmark list by selecting View Bookmarks. This action will display a menu from which you can select to find a particular bookmark or edit a bookmark. It also contains many features that are beyond the scope of this text. The edit bookmark screen is shown in Figure 3-14.

Using the Options submenu

The Options submenu has two primary purposes: to control the screen's appearance and to set default settings for Netscape. We will only consider the first since changing default settings is beyond the scope of this text (and should NOT be done in a classroom environment by anyone other than the local network supervisor).

To control the screen appearance, simply select the Options submenu from the menu bar and note that there is a Preferences command, which is used for default settings, followed by five screen control selections. You can choose to display or not display the Toolbar, Location Window, or the Directory buttons by clicking on the first three options. If an option has a checkmark beside it, then the item will be displayed. You can also control whether images are automatically loaded with a Web page with the fourth option.

The last item in the Options submenu, Save Options, determines whether any changes you make are permanent. Once again, in a classroom environment, you should NOT choose to make any permanent change to the screen's appearance.

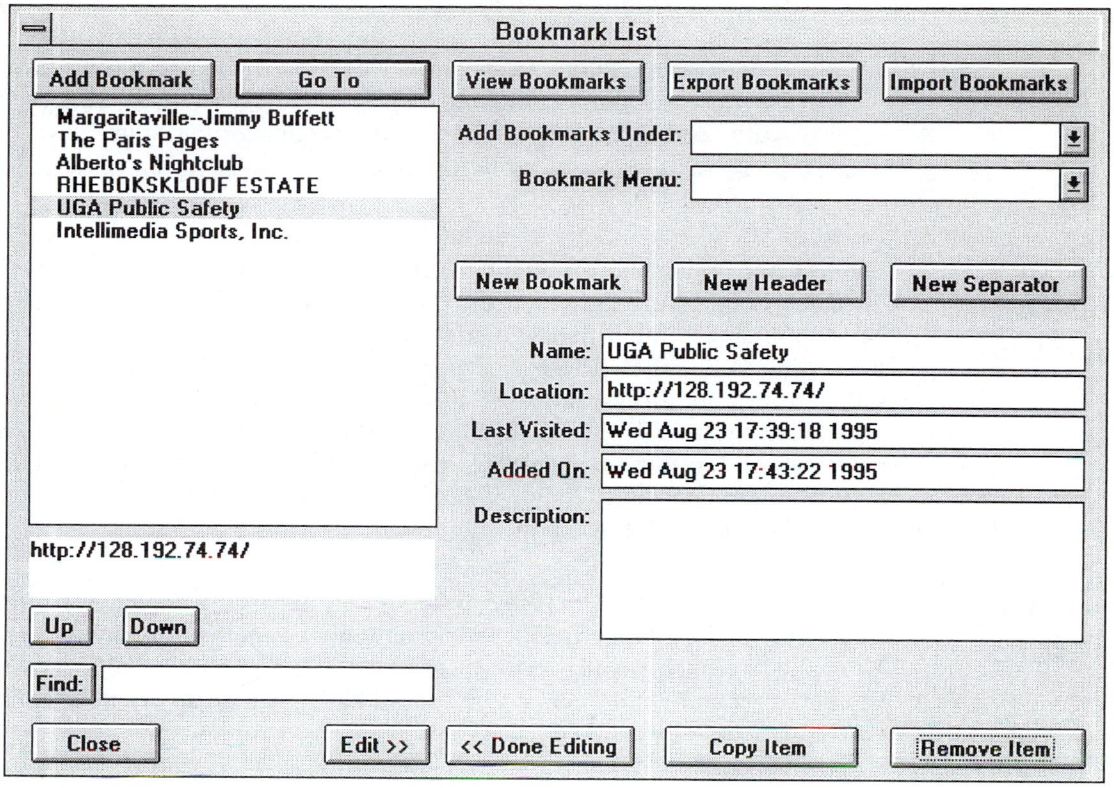

```
┌────────────────────────────────────────────────────────────────────────┐
│ ⊟                              Bookmark List                              │
├────────────────────────────────────────────────────────────────────────┤
│ ┌──────────────┐ ┌──────────────┐  ┌──────────────┐ ┌───────────────┐ ┌───────────────┐ │
│ │ Add Bookmark │ │    Go To     │  │View Bookmarks│ │Export Bookmarks│ │Import Bookmarks│ │
│ └──────────────┘ └──────────────┘  └──────────────┘ └───────────────┘ └───────────────┘ │
│  Margaritaville--Jimmy Buffett      Add Bookmarks Under: ┌───────────────────┐ ▼ │
│  The Paris Pages                                         └───────────────────┘   │
│  Alberto's Nightclub                    Bookmark Menu: ┌───────────────────┐ ▼ │
│  RHEBOKSKLOOF ESTATE                                   └───────────────────┘   │
│  UGA Public Safety                                                              │
│  Intellimedia Sports, Inc.                                                      │
│                                    ┌──────────────┐ ┌────────────┐ ┌──────────────┐ │
│                                    │ New Bookmark │ │ New Header │ │New Separator │ │
│                                    └──────────────┘ └────────────┘ └──────────────┘ │
│                                                                                 │
│                                        Name: │UGA Public Safety            │   │
│                                    Location: │http://128.192.74.74/         │   │
│                                 Last Visited: │Wed Aug 23 17:39:18 1995     │   │
│                                    Added On: │Wed Aug 23 17:43:22 1995     │   │
│                                 Description: ┌─────────────────────────────┐ │
│  http://128.192.74.74/                       │                             │ │
│                                              │                             │ │
│ ┌────┐ ┌──────┐                              └─────────────────────────────┘ │
│ │ Up │ │ Down │                                                              │
│ └────┘ └──────┘                                                              │
│ ┌─────┐┌────────────────┐                                                    │
│ │Find:││                │                                                    │
│ └─────┘└────────────────┘                                                    │
│ ┌───────┐    ┌────────┐  ┌─────────────┐ ┌────────────┐ ┌─────────────┐ │
│ │ Close │    │ Edit >>│  │<< Done Editing│ │ Copy Item │ │ Remove Item │ │
│ └───────┘    └────────┘  └─────────────┘ └────────────┘ └─────────────┘ │
└────────────────────────────────────────────────────────────────────────┘
```

Figure 3-14. Edit bookmark screen

Your turn!

1. Select the Bookmarks submenu and note the listed Web sites. If the current page is not on the bookmark list, add it by selecting the Add Bookmark command.

2. Select the View Bookmarks command and, with highlighting on the current Web page (which you should have added if it were not there), then select the Edit command. You should now see a screen similar to Figure 3-14. Press Esc to return to the Web page.

3. Select the Options submenu and note which items are checked. If the Show Directory Buttons selection is checked, click on it. What happens to the screen's appearance? Now click on this selection again to return the screen to its original appearance. Do the same for the Toolbar and Location selections.

4. If Auto Load Images is checked, click on it to erase the check. Now use the Open button to retrieve the Web page with URL file:///c:\weblearn\albertos\index.htm. Note that no images are displayed. Now use the Images button to display the images. Finally, click on the Auto Load Images selection to return it to its original state.

■ ▬ ▬ ▬ ■ ▬ ▬ ▬ ■ ▬ ▬ ▬ ■ ▬ ▬ ▬ ■ ▬ ▬ ▬ ■ ▬ ▬ ▬ ■

Directory and Help submenus

The last two options on the menu bar are the Directory and Help submenus. These two options are different from the first six in that the submenus do not have commands; rather they provide access to a wide variety of useful and interesting Web pages. These Web pages must be loaded from the Internet rather from a local disk, however. In addition, many of the submenu commands are also available from the Directory buttons, which we discuss in the next section. For these two reasons, we will not consider the Directory and Help menu options here. They will be discussed in Chapter 5, where you will be asked to visit Web sites on the Internet.

Directory buttons

The bottom set of buttons in Netscape are referred to as the **Directory buttons** (see Figure 3-15). These link to a variety of home pages that the developers of Netscape have made available to its users. All of these buttons require you to be able to access the Internet, so you should NOT click on any of them unless your instructor tells you to do so.

Searching for pages

Up to this point, we have demonstrated how to perform all of the browser operations introduced in Chapter 2 except for searching for Web pages on a particular topic. The Net Search Directory button (and the corresponding Directory submenu command) allows you to execute this last browser operation. As with most Netscape operations, you can search for home pages of interest in a number of ways. In this introductory discussion of Netscape, we suggest that you start your search by clicking on the Net Search button in the lower row of buttons. If this is done, the Netscape Search home page is displayed with various search engines listed (you may have to scroll down several lines to find them). We will use the first search engine, InfoSeek Search. To use it, simply type a word or phrase for which you are searching in the space provided and press Enter. For example, if you enter the word "sports," a list of sports-related home pages will be shown.

| What's New! | What's Cool! | Handbook | Net Search | Net Directory | Newsgroups |

Figure 3-15. Directory buttons

You can also search using the Yahoo Directory by clicking Net Directory. This button accesses a database of tens of thousands of Web pages divided into various categories. You can choose to browse through the categories or click on the Yahoo Directory link, select Search from the directory page, and fill in the text box. This short coverage of searching for Internet resources will be expanded in Chapter 5.

Key terms and concepts

content area
directory button
disk cache
location window
memory cache
menu bar
opening home page

point and click navigation
progress bar
security area
shortcut key
status indicator
title bar
toolbar

Exercises

1. List and describe the nine parts of the Netscape screen discussed in the text.

2. List and briefly discuss three ways to access a Web page.

3. What are the three types of buttons on the toolbar. Which button can be used to stop the retrieval of a Web page? Why would this be necessary for a remote Web page but not for a local Web page?

4. What are the four steps that a browser goes through to retrieve a remote Web page? What are the two types of cache that are available with Netscape? Which is permanent?

5. What is a shortcut key in Netscape? What are the three ways to select an option from the menu bar?

6. What are the three ways to make a selection from a drop down submenu in Netscape? Are shortcut keys available for all selections in a drop down submenu?

7. How does the Open File selection from the File submenu differ from the Open Location selection or the Open toolbar button? Can you obtain the same results from the Open Location selection as you do from the Open File selection?

8. For what are Directory buttons used? Why don't we discuss their use with local Web pages?

   For the following seven exercises, you should be working with a computer.

9. Access Netscape. If you do not find the Web Book home page shown in Figure 3-1, press the Home toolbar button. If this does not display the Web Book home page, press the Open toolbar button and enter

the URL:

file:///c:\weblearn\webbook.htm

10. From the Web Book home page, click on Jimmy Buffett's Margaritaville home page hypertext link. What is in the title bar? Click on the clickable map which shows other Web pages? Does the clickable map work? Why or why not?

11. Go to the Margaritaville Store Web page and view the items for sale and the form which is used to order them. Why can't you use this form in local mode? Go back to the Margaritaville home page and go to the last two lines. Click on <u>MARGARITAVILLE</u> to display the outgoing mail message screen. Note the e-mail address and then click on cancel.

12. Go back to the Web Book home page and turn off autoloading of images. Now select the Rhebokskloof Winery home page and note the form in which the page is loaded. Now click on Images. When was the Rhebokskloof Winery founded?

13. Using the Menu bar Options command, turn off display of the Toolbar and the Directory buttons. What happens to the screen? Can you turn off display of the Menu bar? Turn display of the Toolbar and Directory buttons back on.

14. Scroll down to the bottom of the Rhebokskloof Winery home page and use the View menu command to display the source code for this page and then Click on OK. Select one of the Restaurant Web pages from the list of Rhebokskloof pages. Click on the photo of the restaurant to enlarge it. Go back to the Rhebokskloof home page and then visit other Rhebokskloof Web pages.

15. Go back to the Web Book home page and select the home page for Alberto's Nightclub. Use the Find toolbar button to search for occurrences of the word "calendar." How many such occurrences are there on this home page? Scroll down this page and view the image shown there. Use the File Print Preview command to view the form of this page if it were printed.

■ ▬ ■

4   Creating Web Documents

■ ■

Objectives

After completing this chapter, you will be able to:

❖ describe the key features of HTML;

❖ define the difference between logical and physical styles;

❖ define the difference between absolute and relative addressing;

❖ create a Web application using HTML;

❖ understand form and map processing.

What is HTML?

You learned in Chapter 1 that the Web is a client/server system in which the client is called a **browser**. The **server** contains text files that are converted by the browser for display on a monitor. To do this, the browser needs instructions for preparing a text file, instructions which are written in the Hypertext Markup Language **(HTML)**. The basic component of the language is a **tag**, which tells the browser how to display data. For example, the following HTML statement

```
<cite>Computerworld</cite> is a weekly newspaper
for information systems professionals.
```

is displayed as

Computerworld is a weekly newspaper for information systems professionals.

The tags <cite> and </cite> around *Computerworld* inform the browser that this word (i.e., *Computerworld*) must be displayed in citation format (italics in this case). Tags often travel in pairs, encircling the text to be displayed in a particular style. They are almost identical, except for the

75

trailing tag, which has a distinguishing slash (/). As this small example illustrates, HTML is a simple language for describing how a text file will be displayed by a browser, thus explaining the presence of Markup[1] in HTML.

What does the hypertext part of HTML mean? Ordinary text, like this book, is linear; sentences are arranged sequentially, and the author expects that you will read large portions of the text sequentially. Sometimes, as discussed in Chapters 1 and 2, you may want to refer to other parts of the book. Imagine you are reading a sentence containing the acronym HTML, and you don't know what it means. Typically, you would turn to the book's glossary for a definition. Now, imagine you are reading the Web version of this book. When you come across HTML (assuming it is a defined hypertext link), you simply click on the acronym, and the browser retrieves the page containing its definition. After reading the definition, you click on the return icon, a left-pointing arrow, to return to the point where you clicked on HTML. A text that supports electronic linking to other parts of the document or other documents is called **hypertext**. When creating a hypertext document, the author needs to decide which items in a text should be linked to other items, create the link, and then indicate to the reader that a link exists. Creating and denoting a link is easy. The hard part is identifying all the words or phrases that should be linked.

As you are aware from using a browser, a Web document can include **multimedia** objects—images, video, and audio. HTML also includes instructions for defining what type of object to include and where it is stored on the server. There are also features of HTML for handling forms and electronic mail. Because it is possible to define an image as a **hyperlink** (i.e., clicking on the image links you to another page), the term hypermedia is often associated with the HTML.

In summary, HTML is a language for:

1. describing how a Web browser should display a text file retrieved from a server;
2. describing hyperlinks;
3. defining multimedia objects included with a Web document.

You can create a HTML file using any editor or word processor. We will assume that you have access to and are familiar with the editor supplied with your computer's operating system—Write for Windows or SimpleText for Macintosh. Remember to save HTML files as text files.

The form of a HTML document

A HTML document has some standard tags to define its major components. The <html> and </html> tags indicate the beginning and end of a HTML document. The next pair of tags, <head> and </head>, define the document's head which contains the title— indicated by the <title> and </title> tags. The title is displayed in the title bar. Finally, the body of the document lies within the <body> and </body> tags. It is good practice to first define these tags

---

1. Markup is a publishing industry term for describing the size, style, and position of each typographical element on a page.

before writing any other parts of the HTML document. HTML commands to create a simple Web page are shown in Figure 4-1. The resulting Web browser display is illustrated in Figure 4-2. Observe that the title of the document (Web document #1) appears in the title bar.

```
<html>
<head>
<title>Web document #1</title>
</head>
<body>
The body of document #1
</body>
</html>
```

Figure 4-1. HTML to describe a simple Web page

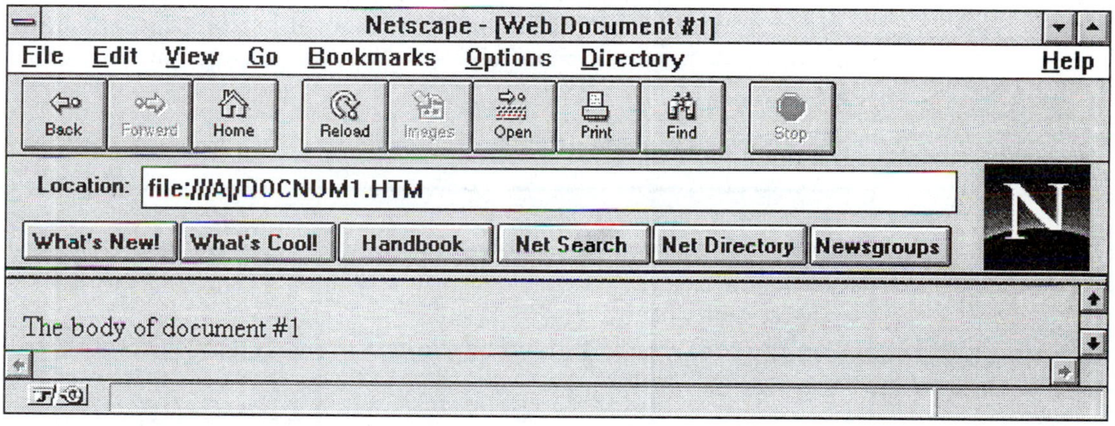

Figure 4-2. A simple Web page

Head

The main element of the head of a HTML document is the title. Each document should have a meaningful title of less than 64 characters. The title, displayed in the title section of the browser's window, should identify a document's content. A meaningful title helps users identify the contents of a page when it is found by a search engine, or appears in a hot list or history list.

Body

The content of a document is contained with the body of a HTML document. The body contains the text and images seen by someone browsing the page. HTML elements define headings, paragraphs, lists, hypertext links, styles, images, and other elements of a document.

Your turn!

1. Use File Manager to copy all the files from the c:\weblearn directory to a floppy disk in the a: drive.

2. Double-click on the Accessories Group box and then double click on the Write[2] icon. In Write, enter the contents of Figure 4-1.

3. Select File Save As... and enter a document name as a:\docnum1.htm. Select the file Type as *.Txt (text file) and click on OK.

4. Click on the down arrowhead to minimize Write and then access Netscape. Click on the Open button and enter the URL as file:/// a:\docnum1.htm The result should look like Figure 4-2.

Headings

Nearly every document uses headings to indicate new sections and subsections. The six heading levels of HTML are labeled h1, h2, ..., h6. As a general rule, use h1 for the main heading, h2 for the next level heading, and so forth for less important headings. The interpretation of heading levels varies by browser, but the presentation in Table 4-1 gives an indication of what you can expect.

Table 4-1: Heading levels

Heading level	Server	Browser
1	`<h1>Heading h1</h1>`	Heading h1
2	`<h2>Heading h2</h2>`	Heading h2
3	`<h3>Heading h3</h3>`	Heading h3
4	`<h4>Heading h4</h4>`	Heading h4
5	`<h5>Heading h5</h5>`	Heading h5
6	`<h6>Heading h6</h6>`	Heading h6

Note: The standard format for illustrating HTML features is to show the HTML commands as stored on the server and the resulting browser display side-by-side under two columns headed *Server* and *Browser*, respectively.

---

2. Use SimpleText for a Macintosh.

Paragraph

The paragraph element, <p>, indicates a paragraph break. Use it to separate two blocks of text, just as you do in standard writing. A paragraph break is not required for headings or list elements.

Line break

The line break element, <br>, indicates the start of a new line. Strictly speaking, it is not the same as a paragraph, but the effect is very similar. Use it for items such as addresses (see Table 4-2).

Table 4-2: A break example

Server	Browser
<address>Athens Webmasters 2357 College Ave Athens, GA 30603</address> 	*Athens Webmasters* *2357 College Ave* *Athens, GA 30603*

Horizontal rule

The horizontal rule, <hr>, is used to draw a horizontal line across a screen. It is a stronger form of text separation than a paragraph break. It can be used at the bottom of a page to separate the details about the owner from the preceding text (see Table 4-3).

Table 4-3: A horizontal rule <hr> example

Server	Browser
<hr>This page is maintained by Fred Bloggs (fredb@meekatharra.au), who is responsible for all errors and omissions.<P>	This page is maintained by Fred Bloggs (fredb@meekatharra.au), who is responsible for all errors and omissions.

Your turn!

1. Click on the down arrowhead to minimize Netscape. Click on the minimized Write icon to maximize Windows Write. If it is not already opened, open the file a:\docnum1.htm.

2. Erase the line in this document: "The body of document #1."

3. Use the H1 heading type to create a new first line of text, "My home page."

4. Use the H2 heading type to create a second line of text "by" followed by your name. For example, the second line of text might read, "by Ned Watson."

5. Use the <hr> tag to create a horizontal line beneath your name.

6. Type your local address (including your e-mail address, if you have one) on the next two or three lines and end each line with the line break <br> tag.

7. Save the new version of a:\docnum1.htm. Minimize Write, maximize Netscape and use the Reload button to bring in the revised version of the Web page.

Now showing at your local Web site

Many movie studios now use the Web to promote new releases. A studio's Web site may contain still photos, interviews with the stars, video clips, games, and contests.

❖ The site for "Batman Forever" presents riddles and supports e-mail to the film's major characters. As you would expect, Batman's butler answers the mail.

❖ You can hike through the forest searching for Pocahontas, John Smith, and Powhatan when you visit Disney's "Pocahontas" Web site.

❖ Visitors to the site for "First Knight" can win private screenings, sweatshirts, books, and posters by answering simple riddles.

The Web enables studios to reach affluent, young, educated males who generally don't read newspapers or watch entertainment shows on TV—an audience who would not normally see traditional movie promotions.

Creation of a Web site is relatively inexpensive, around $100,000, compared to the average of $16 million spent advertising a major film. Furthermore, the Web enables far more information to be presented than other media. A good Web site will not only encourage people to see the movie, but will also promote sales of products associated with the movie.

Adapted from: Y. Arar, Movie promoters find new market on Internet. *Atlanta Journal-Constitution*, July 25, 1995; C3.

HTML style tags

Style tags define how text will appear when displayed by a browser. There are two types of styles applied to groups of characters, words, or sentences: physical and logical. Bold, italics, and underlining are examples of **physical styles**. Emphasis, strong emphasis, and cite are instances of **logical styles**.

Logical and physical styles are used for segments of text within a paragraph. If you wish to apply a logical style to a block of text, you have three choices: preformatted, block quote, and address. For instance, you would use the block quote style to surround a piece of text that is a quote rather than using emphasis. As a result, it is then possible with appropriate software to identify all the quotes in a document by searching for blockquote tags.

Physical styles

Physical styles are illustrated in Table 4-4. The only style that may need additional explanation is <tt> (typewriter), which specifies a monospaced typewriter font, such as Courier. Physical styles should be avoided because some browsers may not handle them.

Table 4-4: Physical styles

Style	Server	Browser
Bold	`<b>Text style</b>`	**Text style**
Italics	`<i>Text style</i>`	*Text style*
Underline	`<u>Text style</u>`	<u>Text style</u>
Typewriter	`<tt>Text style</tt>`	Text style

Logical styles

The usual rendering of logical styles, the preferred form for styles, is shown in Table 4-5. For example, italics are used for emphasis (em). The interpretation of logical styles may not be distinct—emphasis and cite usually display as italics. Some browsers permit customization of logical styles, so you could specify that stronger (strong) will display in purple type.

Table 4-5: Logical styles

Style	Tag	Usual rendering	Server	Browser
Emphasis	em	Italics	`<em>Text style</em>`	*Text style*
Stronger emphasis	strong	Bold	`<strong>Text style</strong>`	**Text style**
Citation	cite	Italics	`<cite>Text style</cite>`	*Text style*
Computer code	code	Monospaced	`<code>Text style</code>`	`Text style`

Preformatted. A block of text, such as computer code, can be displayed in a monospaced font using the <pre> and </pre> tags (see Figure 4-6).

Table 4-6: A preformatted text <pre> example

Server	Browser

```<pre>```
```sum = 0```
```for indx = 1 to 50```
```   sum = sum + obs(indx)```
```next indx```
```</pre>```
	```sum = 0```
	```for indx = 1 to 50```
	``` sum = sum + obs(indx)```
	```next indx```

Block quote. Quoted text is defined using the <blockquote> and </block-quote> tags. A browser may indent or italicize the text. A block quote forces a paragraph break and a blank line before and after the quoted text (see Table 4-7).

Table 4-7: A block quote <block quote> example

Server	Browser

```Groucho Marx:<blockquote>What's```
```a thousand dollars? Mere chicken```
```feed. A poultry matter.```
```</blockquote>```
```In the film, <em>Cocoanuts.</em>```
	Groucho Marx:
	
	  What's a thousand dollars? Mere chicken feed. A poultry matter.
	
	In the film, *Cocoanuts.*

Address. The address mode is normally used for addresses, signatures, and details about the author (see Table 4-8). You will often find this information at the end of a document.

Table 4-8: An address <address> example

Server	Browser

```<address>Richard T. Watson<p>```
```Department of Management<p>```
```University of Georgia<p>```
```Athens, GA 30602-6256</address>```
	Richard T. Watson
	Department of Management
	University of Georgia
	Athens, GA 30602-6256

- -

Your turn!

1. Minimize Netscape, maximize Write, and, if it is not already opened, open the file a:\docnum1.htm in Windows Write.

2. Add a new horizontal line beneath your address.

3. Add a new line to the file starting with the word "Major:" strongly emphasized, followed by your major emphasized. Add a line break tag after this line.

4. Add the Address tag to the two or three lines of your address that you entered earlier.

5. Save the new version of a:\docnum1.htm. Minimize Write, maximize Netscape and use the Reload button to bring in the revised version of the Web page.

Lists

Three types of **lists** can be defined: regular, menu, and descriptive. A regular list is a sequence of paragraphs, a menu list is an interactive menu of choices, and a descriptive list is an inventory of items where each is followed by a descriptive paragraph.

Regular list

A regular list is used for displaying a list of items, which may be bulleted (<ul>) (also known as unordered) or numbered (<ol>) (also known as ordered). A list is surrounded by a pair of tags, and each list element is preceded by a <li> tag (see Table 4-9).

Table 4-9: List examples

Type of list	Server	Browser
UL (unordered)	<ul> <li> Seoul <li> Barcelona <li> Atlanta </ul>	• Seoul • Barcelona • Atlanta
OL (ordered)	<ol> <li> Washington <li> Adams <li> Jefferson </ol>	1. Washington 2. Adams 3. Jefferson

Menu list

A menu list is recommended for situations in which a choice is made from several links. The result is similar to an unordered list (see Table 4-9). Don't be concerned if you don't understand all of the HTML commands used in Table 4-10; they will be covered shortly. The main things to notice are the menu and li tags.

Table 4-10: A menu list example

Server	Browser

`<h2>Useful information for visitors to Paris</h2>`
 	
`<menu>`
 	
`<li> <a href="glossary.html"> Paris glossary</a>`
 	
`<li> <a href="telephone.html"> Telephone</a>`
 	
`</menu>`
	Useful information for visitors to Paris
	
	• <u>Paris glossary</u>
	• <u>Telephone</u>

Descriptive list

A glossary, a good application of a descriptive list, comprises a term and its definition. The example (see Table 4-11) illustrates that <dt> precedes the name of the term and <dd> precedes the definition of the term.

Table 4-11: A descriptive list example

Server	Browser
`<H3>Paris trains</H3>` `<dl>` `<dt><strong>M&eacute;tro</strong>` `<dd>The Paris subway. It is extensive and serves nearly every corner of the city. The last trains are around 00h30.` `<dt><strong>RER</strong>` `<dd>Réseau Express Régional; similar to the Métro except that it also serves the outlying suburbs and regions of Paris. In the center of the city, the distance between RER stations is more significant than for the Métro; an advantage if you want to cover larger distances quickly-even in the center of the city.`  `</dl>`	**Paris trains** Métro The Paris subway. It is extensive and serves nearly every corner of the city. The last trains are around 00h30. RER Réseau Express Régional; similar to the Métro except that it also serves the outlying suburbs and regions of Paris. In the center of the city, the distance between RER stations is more significant than for the Métro; an advantage if you want to cover larger distances quickly-even in the center of the city.

■ ■

Your turn!

1. Minimize Netscape, maximize Write, and, if it is not already opened, open the file a:\docnum1.htm.

2. Beneath the line that displays your major, add a new line "Favorite Courses" that is underlined. End the line with a line break tag.

3. Add an ordered list of the three or four favorite courses that you have taken in your college career. (Naturally, you will want to include the current course!)

4. Add a new line "Other Courses" that is underlined with a line break.

5. Add an unordered list of three or four other courses that you have taken in your college career.

6. Save the new version of a:\docnum1.htm. Minimize Write, maximize Netscape and use the Reload button to bring in the revised version of the Web page.

■ ■

Anchors and images

The use of hyperlinks and hypermedia makes the Web easy to navigate and visually stimulating. These two features, easily implemented using HTML, are the focus of this section.

The **anchor tag** pair is the cornerstone of HTML's hypertext capabilities. It indicates the name of an object to be retrieved by the browser from a server. The object can be another Web document or some text within the current Web page. The anchor structure is also used to support e-mail. Mastering the use of anchors is critical to the creation of a link within and between Web pages. Every anchor has four components (see Figure 4-3). All anchors begin with "<a" and end with "</a>." An anchor specifies the address of the document or text to be retrieved, with the format varying with the type of anchor. Finally, an anchor usually has associate text to indicate the result of clicking on the link.

A major benefit of hypertext is that you can decompose a large linear document into smaller, logical chunks that can be reached using hyperlinks. There are two approaches to creating these logical chunks. First, you can keep the text as one physical file and create destination points within the text (linking within a document). Alternatively, you can make each logical chunk a separate file with a unique URL (linking to another document). Also, you can have a combination of these two approaches (linking to a destination within another document). These three approaches result in three different formats for anchors with a type of href. A fourth href format is used for e-mail and can be thought of as linking to a person.

The other anchor type, name, is used to name a destination point within a document. It has to be a different type (name instead of href) so that a browser can distinguish between a destination and a link.

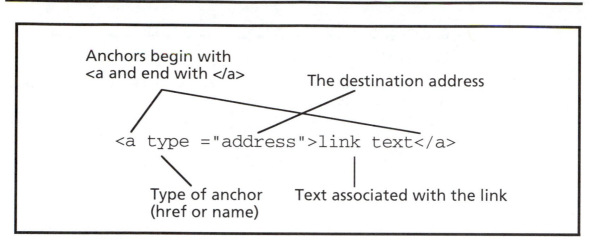

Figure 4-3. Components of an anchor

Table 4-12: The href type anchors

Type	Format
Linking within a document	`<a href="#identifier">link text</a>`
Linking to another document	`<a href="URL">link text</a>`
Linking to a destination within another document	`<a href="URL#identifier">link text</a>`
Sending e-mail	`<a href="mailto:e-mail address">link text</a>`

Table 4-13: The name type anchor

Type	Format
Destination point within a document	`<a name="#identifier">destination text</a>`

Linking within a document

Dividing a document into named destination points makes it possible to link to a place within the same document. Although any place within a document can be a destination point, it is generally a heading or subheading. Consider the case in which the document begins with a table of contents, a common use of links within a document (see Figure 4-14). The name of each destination point is preceded by a #. In this case, *leftbank* is the name of the destination point.

Every destination point must be uniquely labeled, and accompanied by a corresponding HTML code to denote it. Within the document, the name[3] ref-

---

3. More recent specifications of HTML are likely to use id rather than name, but this should not cause any problems.

Table 4-14: Linking within a document

Server	Browser

`<menu>`
 	
`<li><a href="#leftbank">Left Bank</a>`
 	
...
 	
`</menu>`
 	
...
 	
`<strong> <a name="#leftbank">Left Bank (Rive Gauche)</a></strong>•`
	• <u>Left Bank</u>
	
	...
	
	Left Bank (Rive Gauche)

erence <a name="#leftbank"> denotes the destination point of a link.Thus if you click on <u>Left Bank</u> in the menu (the href anchor), the browser will jump to the text beginning **Left Bank (Rive Gauche)**, the name anchor. You can have many href anchors linking to one name anchor, but every name anchor must be unique, or the browser will be confused.

Linking to another document

To create a link to another page, simply specify the URL. If the page is on another Web server, then the full URL must be given. Specifying the full URL is called absolute addressing. The first example in Figure 4-15 illustrates use of **absolute addressing**.

Table 4-15: Linking to other documents

Type of addressing	Server	Browser
Absolute	`<a href="http://www.uga.edu/">` `University of Georgia</a>`	<u>University of Georgia</u>
Relative	`<a href="wineshop.htm">` `Wine Shop</a>`	<u>Wine Shop</u>
Relative	`<a href= "../Rhebok/winery.htm">` `Rhebokskloof Estate</a>`	<u>Rhebokskloof Estate</u>

If the file is on the same server, then only the path portion of the URL should be specified. This is called *relative addressing*. The second example in Table 4-15 demonstrates relative addressing where the desired document is in the same directory as the current document. The example describes a situation where the current document, main.htm, and the document it references, books.htm, are both in the Paris directory (see Figure 4-4).

The third example in Table 4-15 illustrates **relative addressing** where the document to be retrieved is in another directory on the same server. The ".." indicates a path relative to the root directory for the server. The example

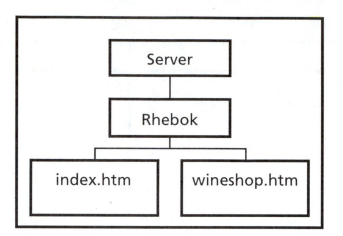

Figure 4-4. Relative addressing within the same directory

describes a situation where the current document, food.htm, and the document it references, winery.htm, are in different directories (see Figure 4-5).

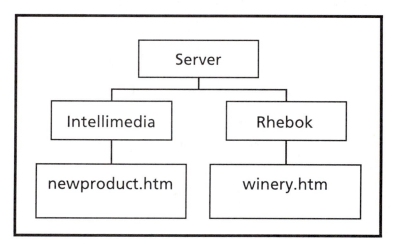

Figure 4-5. Relative addressing within the same server

Relative addressing should be used whenever possible because it makes HTML files transportable. If absolute addressing is used for every anchor, then moving a set of HTML files to another server can mean extensive editing (e.g., changing every occurrence of www.widget.com to www.thing.com in every HTML file); relative addressing will mean very few changes.

Linking to a destination point within another document

To link to specific points within another document, combine the principles of linking between and within documents. The following anchor illustrates a link from another server to www.cba.uga.edu and then to a particular point within a document:

```
<a href="http://www.cba.uga.edu/management/
phd.html#courses"> University of Georgia,
Ph. D. in Management courses</a>
```

The browser first finds the named server (www.cba.uga.edu), locates the desired document on that server (management/phd.html), searches for <a name="#courses"> within that document, and then displays the document starting at that location.

Your turn!

1. Minimize Netscape, maximize Write, and, if it is not already opened, open the file a:\docnum1.htm.

2. Beneath the first horizontal line tag on this page, insert a level three heading "Parts of my page" and then use the menu tag to create a table of contents for your Web page.

3. Your menu should show two choices: Personal Information and School Information. The Personal Information choice should be linked to your address information, and the School Information choice should be linked to your major and course information.

4. Create a link to a document on the server set up to support this book. The URL of this document is http://www.negia.net/~webbook and it has useful information about the authors of this book.

5. Save the new version of a:\docnum1.htm. Minimize Write, maximize Netscape, and use the Reload button to bring in the revised version of the Web page.

6. Click on each of the links you created to determine if your links are working correctly. Use the Back button to return to the original location in the Web page.

Linking to e-mail

Some browsers (e.g., Netscape) incorporate an e-mail link. Imagine that you place your resume on the Web, and you want to ensure that potential employers can contact you. In addition to giving your phone number, you may want to also state your e-mail address. Even better, set up an e-mail link so that commencing communication requires just a single click (see Table 4-16).

When the e-mail link is selected, a message window appears (see Figure 4-6). The browser inserts the sender's address information in the From field (this information must have been previously defined), and the receiver's e-

Table 4-16: An e-mail link

Server	Browser
`For further information, e-mail <a href="mailto:president@whitehouse.gov>" The President</a>`	For further information, e-mail <u>The President</u>

mail address in the Mail to field. The sender then completes the rest of the message and clicks on the Send button. Recall that, although you send mail from a browser, you cannot read it with a browser, although this limitation should disappear with later releases.

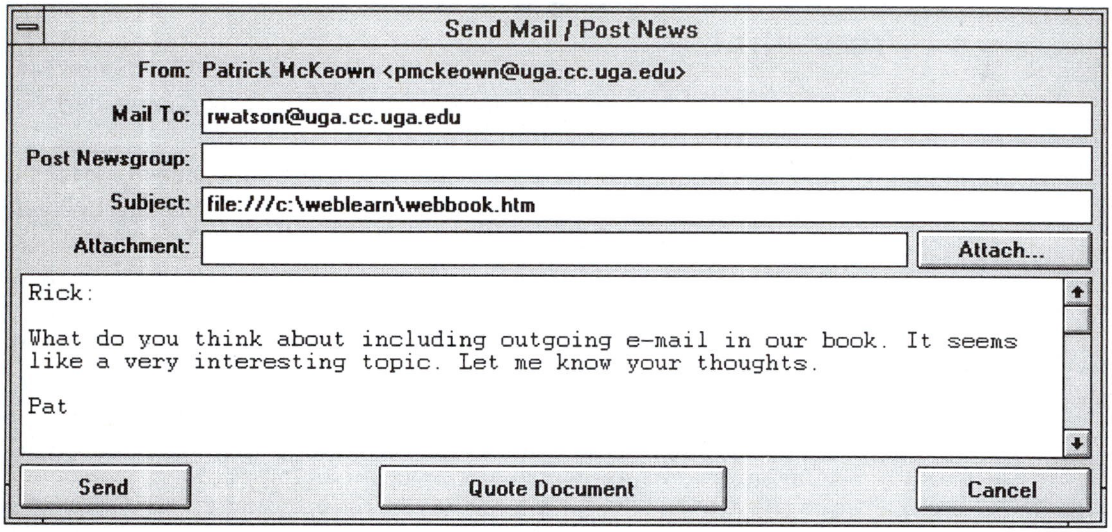

```
┌─────────────────────────────────────────────────────────────┐
│ ─│              Send Mail / Post News                        │
├─────────────────────────────────────────────────────────────┤
│      From:  Patrick McKeown <pmckeown@uga.cc.uga.edu>        │
│    Mail To: │rwatson@uga.cc.uga.edu                       │  │
│ Post Newsgroup: │                                        │  │
│    Subject: │file:///c:\weblearn\webbook.htm             │  │
│  Attachment: │                                    │ Attach... ││
├─────────────────────────────────────────────────────────────┤
│ Rick:                                                     ↑ │
│                                                             │
│ What do you think about including outgoing e-mail in our book. It seems │
│ like a very interesting topic. Let me know your thoughts.  │
│                                                             │
│ Pat                                                       ↓ │
├─────────────────────────────────────────────────────────────┤
│   ┌────────┐        ┌──────────────────┐      ┌──────────┐  │
│   │  Send  │        │  Quote Document  │      │  Cancel  │  │
│   └────────┘        └──────────────────┘      └──────────┘  │
└─────────────────────────────────────────────────────────────┘
```

Figure 4-6. A message window

Loading an image

Images make Web pages interesting. A corporate logo, picture of a building, or a map can often explain far more than pages of text. Images are stored in a format that can be read by the browser. Files stored in the most popular formats, GIF and JPEG, are easily identified by the file extensions of gif and jpeg (jpe or jpg for Windows).

If you have an image file in gif or jpeg format, then it is very easy to write the HTML to display the image (see Figure 4-7). The image tag starts with the identifier, img scr=, to indicate an image is being defined. Next comes the URL of the file. The final component is the optional alignment specification-- text that is associated with the image but aligned with the bottom (the default), middle, or top of the image.

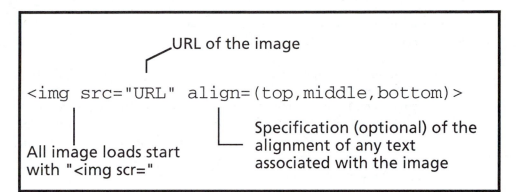

Figure 4-7. HTML for image loading

The example in Table 4-17 shows the effect of each of the alignment options. In the first case, there is no associated text. The other three examples illustrate the use of top, middle, and bottom alignment.

Table 4-17:

Browser	Server
`<img src=infoicon.gif>`	
`<h1><img src=infoicon.gif align=top> Paris Visitors' Center </h1>`	**Paris Visitors' Center**
`<h1><img src=infoicon.gif align=middle> Paris Visitors' Center </h1>`	**Paris Visitors' Center**
`<h1><img src=infoicon.gif align=bottom> Paris Visitors' Center </h1>`	**Paris Visitors' Center**

Your turn!

1. Minimize Netscape, maximize Write, and, if it is not already opened, open the file a:\docnum1.htm. At the very beginning of your Web page, create an image link to the file metamorp.gif found in c:\weblearn. Place the label "Metamorphosis" at the top of the image.

2. Save the new version of a:\docnum1.htm. Minimize Write, maximize Netscape, and use the Reload button to bring in the revised version of the Web page. Note the placement of the image and label.

Digital literacy

The traditional notion of literacy—the ability to read and write—is being extended to mean the capacity to understand information in whatever form it is presented—text, recorded sounds, images, or video. To be literate in a digital world means one has the skills to decipher complex images and sounds as well as the subtleties of the written word. A digitally literate person can make sense of a mixture of words, images, and sounds. A person who is highly literate in a digital world has the combined skills of a book reviewer, art critic, movie fan, and music lover.

Print captures words permanently, but multimedia is volatile. Today's Web page may be quite different from yesterday's. Graphics may be altered continually and text revised. Print is static—for all time; multimedia is dynamic—for the present.

Printing and books are intimately tied to the idea of intellectual property. Ideas are fixed in type and can therefore be sold and owned. But what happens when ideas are not fixed and are frequently modified or even radically altered? Digital literacy is more like speaking than writing—the originator can elaborate, change, and revise ideas in a dynamic dialogue with many readers.

Digital literature will become an art form. We will extol some pages for their artistic blend of multimedia. There may be the equivalent of the Oscar or Nobel Prize for the very best Web works.

Adapted from: Lanham, R. A. Digital literacy: multimedia will require equal facility in word, image, and sound. *Scientific American*. 1995; 273 (3): 198, 200.

Advanced features

The usefulness of a HTML document often can be enhanced by tables, forms, or maps. **Tables** make sets of data more readable; **forms** are the basis of many interactive applications (e.g., taking customers' orders); and **maps** are navigational aids. In addition, **special characters** improve the readability of documents because they permit the representation of characters such as é and ã.

Tables

The table markup commands, introduced in HTML 3.0, support the presentation of a table containing a caption, column and row headers, and cell elements. An example of the markup language (see Figure 4-8) and resulting browser display (see Figure 4-9) demonstrates the use of table markup commands.

```
<table border>
<Caption>Average daily maximum and minimum temperatures</caption>
<th> Month <th> Max (F) <th> Max (C) <th> Min (F) <th> Min (C) <tr>
<td> January <td> 43 <td> 6 <td> 34 <td> 1 <tr>
<td> February <td> 45 <td> 7 <td> 34 <td> 1 <tr>
<td> March <td> 54 <td> 12 <td> 39 <td> 4 <tr>
<td> April <td> 60 <td> 16 <td> 43 <td> 6 <tr>
<td> May <td> 68 <td> 20 <td> 49 <td> 9 <tr>
<td> June <td> 73 <td> 23 <td> 55 <td> 13 <tr>
<td> July <td> 76 <td> 24 <td> 58 <td> 14 <tr>
<td> August <td> 75 <td> 24 <td> 58 <td> 14 <tr>
<td> September <td> 76 <td> 24 <td> 53 <td> 12 <tr>
<td> October <td> 60 <td> 16 <td> 46 <td> 8 <tr>
<td> November <td> 50 <td> 10 <td> 40 <td> 4 <tr>
<td> December <td> 44 <td> 7 <td> 36 <td> 2 <tr>
</table>
```

Figure 4-8. Server definition of a table

A table definition is enclosed by the tags <table border> and </table>. The <caption> and </caption> tags surround a table's caption. A column or row heading is preceded by a <th> tag. For instance, "<th> Month" indicates that Month is a heading cell (a column heading in this case because it follows the table's caption). The <td> tag precedes a cell's data (e.g., <td> March). The end of each row is signified by a <tr> tag. The relatively simple HTML commands create a pleasing presentation.

Use a spreadsheet to speed up the preparation of a table definition. For example, the table definition shown in Table 4-8 was created by setting up a spreadsheet with 11 columns (see Figure 4-10). After entering the <td> and

Temperatures

Average daily maximum and minimum temperatures

Month	Max (F)	Max (C)	Min (F)	Min (C)
January	43	6	34	1
February	45	7	34	1
March	54	12	39	4
April	60	16	43	6
May	68	20	49	9
June	73	23	55	13
July	76	24	58	14
August	75	24	58	14
September	76	24	53	12
October	60	16	46	8
November	50	10	40	4
December	44	7	36	2

Figure 4-9. Browser display of a table

<tr> tags in the second row, use the fill down command to enter the remaining tags. Then, complete data entry, and cut-and-paste the table into your editor. Of course, we were extra smart in this case. We used a formula to convert Fahrenheit to Celsius.

<th>	Month	<th>	Max (F)	<th>	Max(C)	<th>	Min(F)	<th>	Min(C)	<tr>
<td>	January	<td>	4 3	<td>	6	<td>	3 4	<td>	1	<tr>
<td>	February	<td>	4 5	<td>	7	<td>	3 4	<td>	1	<tr>
<td>	March	<td>	5 4	<td>	1 2	<td>	3 9	<td>	4	<tr>
<td>	April	<td>	6 0	<td>	1 6	<td>	4 3	<td>	6	<tr>
<td>	May	<td>	6 8	<td>	2 0	<td>	4 9	<td>	9	<tr>
<td>	June	<td>	7 3	<td>	2 3	<td>	5 5	<td>	1 3	<tr>
<td>	July	<td>	7 6	<td>	2 4	<td>	5 8	<td>	1 4	<tr>
<td>	August	<td>	7 5	<td>	2 4	<td>	5 8	<td>	1 4	<tr>
<td>	September	<td>	7 6	<td>	2 4	<td>	5 3	<td>	1 2	<tr>
<td>	October	<td>	6 0	<td>	1 6	<td>	4 6	<td>	8	<tr>
<td>	November	<td>	5 0	<td>	1 0	<td>	4 0	<td>	4	<tr>
<td>	December	<td>	4 4	<td>	7	<td>	3 6	<td>	2	<tr>

Figure 4-10. Using a spreadsheet for table definition

Forms

Interactive Web applications can be created using HTML's form definition commands. Although it is very easy to create a form, processing it requires considerably more skill because each form needs a corresponding application to process its data. When a completed form is submitted, the data are sent to the Web server, which simply passes the data on to an application specifically built for handling the form (see Figure 4-11). After processing the data, the form handler returns a response to the Web server (e.g., Thank you for your order), which is then sent to the browser for display. A form handler application is written using a language such as C. Because you need programming skills to process forms, we will not cover the HTML for forms design.

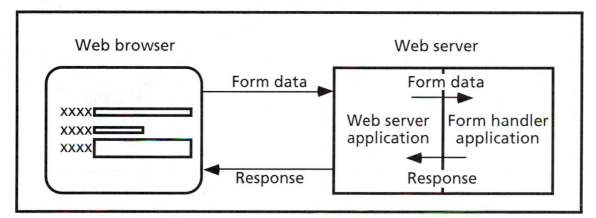

Figure 4-11. Processing a form

Maps

A map is an interesting alternative to a menu of links.[4] Instead of clicking on the text of a link, the user clicks on a region of an image, which can be rectangular, circular, oval, or irregular. Because the image is graphically active, the server can interpret the click and take action, such as linking to another page. Any image can be converted to an active map. Defining a map requires specifying the URL of the map processing application, the name of the map definition file, and adding the ismap key word to the img command, as shown below:

```
<a href="mapserve.acgi$paris.map"><img
    src="parismap.gif" ismap></a>
```

When you click the mouse on a region of a map (parismap.gif in the preceding example), the browser sends the server the coordinates of the mouse's pointer. The server then passes these coordinates to the map processing application (mapserve.acgi), which determines the action to take based on the coordinates received (see Figure 4-12).

---

4. For some good examples, see http://www.uwtc.washington.edu/Computing/WWW/ Map.html.

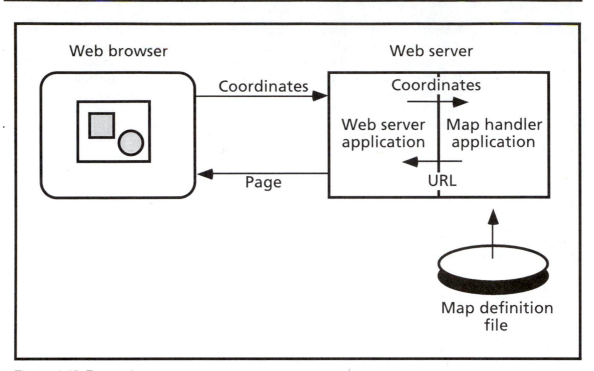

Figure 4-12. Processing a map

A map application requires a map definition file (paris.map in the preceding example), which defines the active regions of a map. A map definition file is a text file containing a line for each region. For rectangular regions, the line contains the top left and bottom right coordinates. For a circular region, the line contains the coordinates of the center and one edge to determine the radius of the circle. Ovals are defined by the rectangle that bounds them. Irregular regions are described by the x,y coordinates for each vertex. The coordinates of a region on a map can be readily determined using special software that displays the coordinates of any point on a graphic. The top-left corner of a map is defined as (0,0) and each pixel represents one coordinate unit (see Figure 4-13).

Special characters

You have already seen some examples of special characters in HTML (e.g., é in Métro). These special characters are defined using the general format &charactername; where charactername is descriptive of the character (e.g., é for é). Note the use of & and ; to indicate the beginning and end of the definition of a special character. Because &, <, and, > have a special meaning within HTML, these characters must be represented as special characters (see Table 4-18). Appendix A contains a complete listing of special characters.

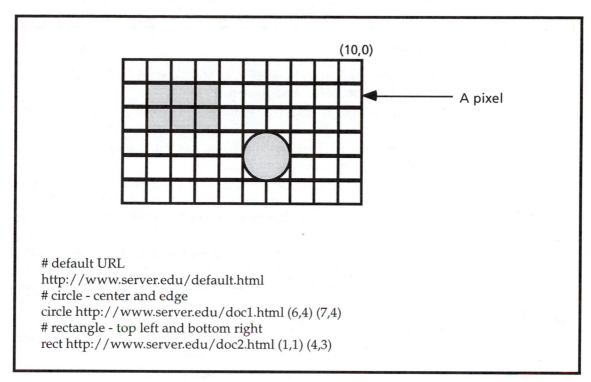

```
# default URL
http://www.server.edu/default.html
# circle - center and edge
circle http://www.server.edu/doc1.html (6,4) (7,4)
# rectangle - top left and bottom right
rect http://www.server.edu/doc2.html (1,1) (4,3)
```

Figure 4-13. A map with its definition file

Table 4-18: Some special characters

Server	Browser
&	&
<	<
>	>
é	é

Key terms and concepts

absolute addressing
anchor
browser
form
HTML
hypermedia
hypertext
list
logical style
map

markup language
multimedia
physical style
relative addressing
server
special character
style tag
table
tag

Exercises

1. Create a page describing yourself. Make certain you include the capability for people to send you e-mail.

2. Add some links from your home page to some of your favorite Web sites.

3. Modify your home page so that you can link to text within it (i.e., try linking within a document).

4. Write a description of a friend. Use appropriate logical styles to emphasize some key attributes of your friend. Using appropriate HTML coding, include a common phrase or remark you often hear your friend say.

5. Pretend that you are a famous writer of detective novels. Write a description of yourself, and include the names and details of two books you have written. Use headings to separate the different parts of the text.

6. Two other HTML styles are center and blink. Write HTML code to discover the effect of these commands. (Hint: the first pair of each tags are <center> and <blink>, respectively.)

7. Create a standard set of HTML code to be placed at the bottom of each document you create.

8. Strikethrough, superscript, and subscript are physical styles with leading tags <s>, <sup>, and <sub>, respectively. Write HTML to investigate how text formatted with these styles is displayed.

9. Write HTML to list the names of five capital cities in Europe.

10. The five largest cities in France are: Paris 2,152,000; Marseilles 801,000; Lyon 415,000; Toulouse 359,000; Nice 342,000 (1990 estimates). Write HTML to show these cities ranked by size; display the population as well as the city's name.

5   Web Searching and other Internet Resources

- -

Objectives

After completing this chapter, you will be able to:

❖ use Web search engines and directories;

❖ use other Internet resources in conjunction with the Web;

❖ describe some of the major methods of electronic information exchange;

❖ explain why encryption is needed, and the principles of public key encryption.

Introduction

In earlier chapters, you learned the basics of Web navigation using Web documents stored on a local disk. Now it is time to leave the nest and venture onto the Web itself. In this chapter, you will access Web sites throughout the world. The URL of each mentioned site is listed in the footnote. To make life easier, all of these sites, and some other interesting places, are listed at one Web site.[1] Thus, you can type the URL of each site or connect to the central listing.

Now that you can access the full resources of the Web, you need to learn how to find information. This chapter is divided into two major sections, each distinguished by a dominant headline. The first section covers methods for searching the Web. The Web is not the only Internet resource, and some other very useful Internet features are covered in the second section.

---

1. http://www.negia.net/~webbook

Finding Web resources

By now you will have realized that the Web contains a tremendous variety of useful information. But, how do you find things? Fortunately, because all Internet resources are stored in electronic format, we can use computers to help us search for information.

Directory buttons

Netscape's **directory** buttons (see Figure 5-1), which were briefly mentioned in Chapter 3, are a good place to start when seeking information. Each of these buttons is now discussed, with the exception of *Newsgroups*, which is considered in the section on Usenet news. Remember, you will need Web access to explore personally any of these buttons.

| What's New! | What's Cool! | Handbook | Net Search | Net Directory | Newsgroups |

Figure 5-1. Directory buttons

What's New

The What's New page, maintained by Netscape, lists some recent additions that illustrate advanced features of the Web or are particularly innovative. The explosive growth of the Web means that this can be only a sample of new pages. If you are looking for imaginative and resourceful uses of the Web, this is a good place to start.

What's Cool?

What's Cool is a list of pages that Netscape classifies as cool. As Shakespeare might have said: "Methinks cool is in the brain of the browser." Again, if you are looking for some fresh ideas, check out What's Cool.

Handbook

On-line help for Netscape is just a click away with the *Handbook* button, which contains a tutorial, reference, and index. The tutorial teaches the basic Netscape commands, explains elementary Internet concepts, and provides lessons for learning Netscape. The reference section overviews the items of the Netscape interface, describes each menu item, and answers some common questions on the use of Netscape. Finally, the index is a readily accessed reference to Netscape functions and features. If you need to learn more about Netscape, then read the Handbook.

Net Search

Net Search is very handy when you are trying to find pages on a particular topic. Imagine you are planning a trip to Bermuda and would like to read some tourist information before deciding where to stay and what to do. Try using Net Search, which gives you access to the InfoSeek **search engine**. You can then search for pages containing the keyword *Bermuda* (see Figure 5-2).

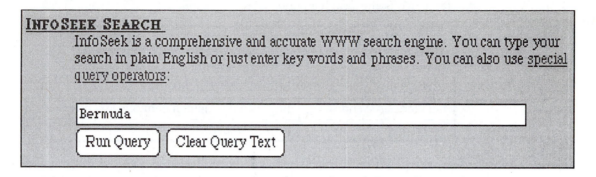

Figure 5-2. A search request

A successful search returns a list of Web sites matching the keyword. In this case, the partial results of the search (see Figure 5-3) provide links to two Web sites containing details of Bermuda. Another couple of clicks and you will be in Bermuda—virtually. Happy holiday!

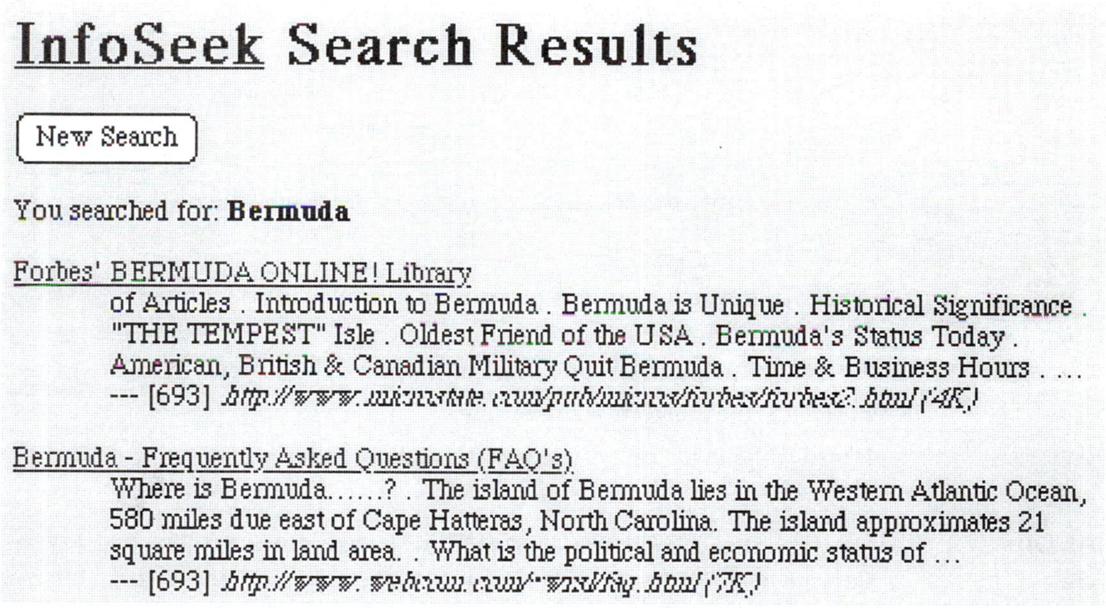

InfoSeek Search Results

New Search

You searched for: **Bermuda**

Forbes' BERMUDA ONLINE! Library
of Articles . Introduction to Bermuda . Bermuda is Unique . Historical Significance .
"THE TEMPEST" Isle . Oldest Friend of the USA . Bermuda's Status Today .
American, British & Canadian Military Quit Bermuda . Time & Business Hours . ...
--- [693] *http://www.microstate.com/pub/microstate/forbes/forbes2.html (4K)*

Bermuda - Frequently Asked Questions (FAQ's)
Where is Bermuda......? . The island of Bermuda lies in the Western Atlantic Ocean,
580 miles due east of Cape Hatteras, North Carolina. The island approximates 21
square miles in land area. . What is the political and economic status of ...
--- [693] *http://www.webrum.com/~world/faq.html (7K)*

Figure 5-3. A search report

There are a number of search engines available. If you find Net Search is slow because of Web traffic or it does not give you a relevant list of pages, then try one of the other search engines (see Table 5-1). Some search tools have additional helpful features. For example, EINet Galaxy gives you a choice of documents types to search (e.g., Gopher, Web page contents, or Web page titles).

Table 5-1: Some search engines

Name	URL
EINet Galaxy	http://www.einet.net/search.html
Lycos	http://lycos.cs.cmu.edu/
net.Genesis Wandex	http://www.netgen.com/cgi/wandex
WebCrawler	http://webcrawler.com/

Searching tips. Not all search engines work the same way, but there are some basic search specification concepts that should work for your favorite search engine.

✤ A simple keyword search
   rock music
   will identify pages containing *either* the word "rock" or "music."

✤ Boolean query
   rock AND music
   will identify pages containing *both* the words "rock" and "music."

✤ Phrase query
   "rock music"
   will identify pages containing the phrase "rock music."

✤ Complex query
   Elvis AND "rock music"
   will identify pages containing the word Elvis and the phrase "rock music."

If your search does not produce many relevant documents, try some of the following tactics:

✤ read the help screens and searching tips for the search engine;

✤ specify the search more precisely;

✤ use AND to narrow the search (OR will broaden it).

Net Directory

An alternative search strategy is to link to **Yahoo** by clicking Net Directory. Yahoo is a directory of Web sites listed by major categories (e.g., business), with each category further broken down into sub-categories (e.g., marketing) which may be further subdivided into topics. Other directories are available (see Table 5-2). The net.Genesis Wandex directory lets you search by domain name (e.g., you can get a complete list of Norwegian pages by specifying a domain name of *no*).

Let's say you have an all-abiding interest in Australian Rules Football (the game for real men without helmets and padding). You can use Yahoo to find home pages dealing with this subject. The major category is Recreation, sub-category Sports, and topic Football (Australian). If you select the first option

Table 5-2: Some directories

Name	URL
EINet Galaxy	http://www.einet.net/galaxy.html
net.Genesis Wandex	http://www.netgen.com/cgi/comprehensive

on the list (1995 AFL), you will discover that Carlton—the mighty Blues—won the 1995 grand final.

Tactics for keeping current

It is impossible for anyone to keep track of Web development. There are just too many new pages being added and many existing pages are continually being revised. The great advantage of the Web—the ease with which pages can be created and maintained—also causes two major problems. First, how do you find information? Second, how do you make certain people can find your home page?

The first problem was addressed earlier in this section. Use search engines or directories to find pages that match your interests. Once you have found pages that are likely to be of continuing interest, make them bookmarks. For instance, if you are a sports fan, you might want to add ESPNet[2] to your list of bookmarks. Commonly used directories are also good candidates for bookmarks.

Once you have added a few bookmarks, you will find scanning of the bookmark list somewhat tedious. Fortunately, Netscape allows you to create a hierarchical directory of personal bookmarks. You can collect all your leisure interest pages, in alphabetical order, under the heading *Leisure*.

Getting people to find your home page, the second problem, is a particularly important issue for businesses. There is not much sense advertising on the Web if very few people visit your home page. As you would expect, there are several tools for registering your page with search engines and directories. Even better, there is a Web site that facilitates mass registration,[3] so that you can quickly transmit the URL and descriptive keywords of your page to the major search engines and directories. Registering your page is not just for organizations; anyone can do it. If you develop some pages describing a particular event (e.g., recorded sightings of Elvis) or hobby, then register it so that anyone else with a similar interest can find your work.

Another useful technique for keeping current is *Frequently Asked Questions—FAQs* (pronounced *facks*). Many Web visitors, and indeed some users of other software, often ask the same questions. Consequently, some Web sites keep track of these questions and list them with a corresponding response. Skimming through the FAQs is an efficient means of discovering the features and limitations of a Web site or a piece of software. To see one use of FAQs, check the results of the Bermuda search (Figure 5-3)

---

2. http://espnet.sportszone.com

3. http://www.cen.uiuc.edu/~banister/submit-it/

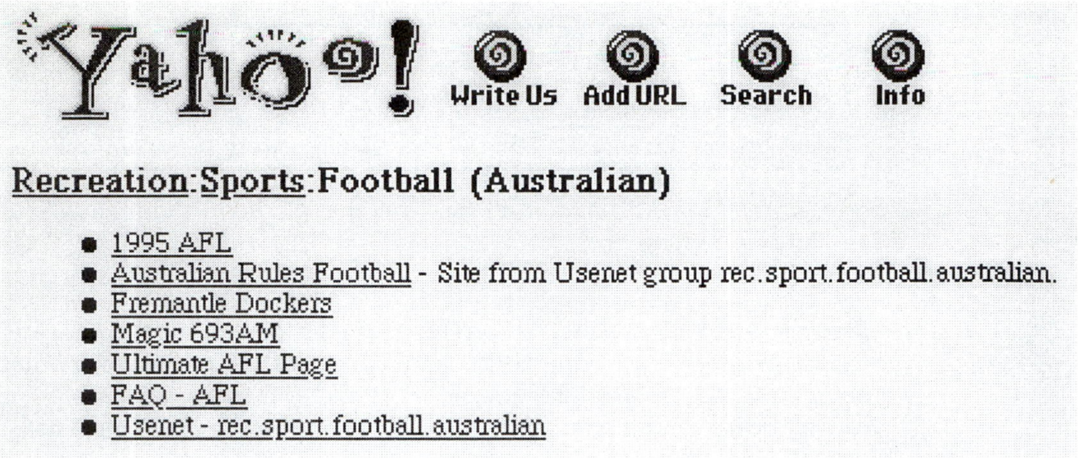

Yahoo!
Write Us
Add URL
Search
Info
Recreation:Sports:Football (Australian)
1995 AFL
Australian Rules Football - Site from Usenet group rec.sport.football.australian.
Fremantle Dockers
Magic 693AM
Ultimate AFL Page
FAQ - AFL
Usenet - rec.sport.football.australian

Figure 5-4. Yahoo directory example

Your turn!

1. Use Net Search to find information on the place you would most like to visit on your next vacation.
2. Repeat the previous exercise, using Net Directory. Which search was more successful? How easy was it to use each tool?

The Web—the mother of all Internet resources

The Web is a general interface to many other Internet resources. For example, a Web browser can retrieve and display Gopher documents and download anonymous FTP files. Thus, once you have learned how to use a Web browser, you have access to many other Internet resources. In this section, we describe some other Internet resources and illustrate how to use HTML to access these resources from within a Web application (see Figure 5-5) using a browser or from within a Web application, respectively.

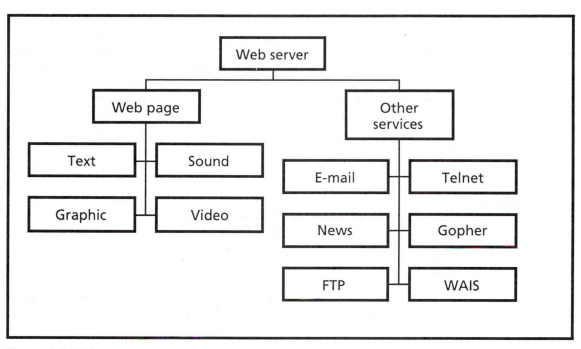

Figure 5-5. Web services

Electronic mail

E-mail, discussed in Chapters 2 and 4, is one of the most popular uses of the Internet, and we assume you have ready access to e-mail software and know how to use it. However, if you are unfamiliar with communicating via e-mail, we suggest that you read some advice on e-mail communication.[4]

Directories— finding someone

As you will recall from the discussion of e-mail in earlier chapters, you need to know the intended receiver's e-mail address before you can communicate. Finding an Internet address is not as simple as dialing the telephone company's directory service or flipping through the telephone book. Because Internet is a loose federation of networks, there is no central registry of addresses. Fortunately, the Internet contains several databases that house information about individuals. A good starting point is World Phonebooks at Texas Tech University,[5] which contains links to a variety of **electronic phonebooks**. Searching is not as simple as it could be since there are several directories from which to select and often you need to interface with a not very friendly UNIX server to specify your search. Nevertheless, if you are trying to find someone's e-mail address, the directories are worth trying.

---

4. http://galaxy.einet.net/galaxy/Business-and-Commerce/
   Management/Communications/How_to_Improve_Your_E_Mail.html
5. gopher://cs4sun.cs.ttu.edu/11/Phone%20Books

If you know where that person works, then another approach is to use a search engine (discussed earlier in this chapter) to find the organization's home page and look for the electronic phonebook. For example, the University of Georgia's home page[6] contains a link to its phonebook, and you can search for anyone connected with the university (faculty, staff, and students).

Most e-mail address search facilities have a familiar Web interface and use forms for specifying details of the person sought. Once you have located the phonebook, you enter the person's name (see Figure 5-6), and a few seconds later, you get information such as the person's postal address, phone number, and e-mail address.

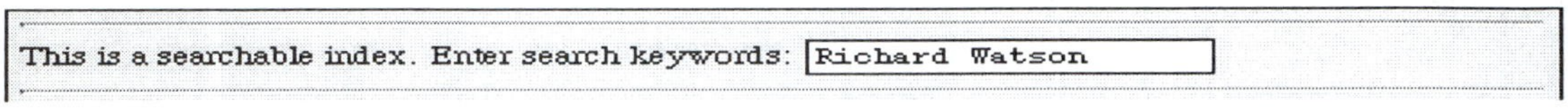

This is a searchable index. Enter search keywords: `Richard Watson`

Figure 5-6. A phonebook search request

Your turn!

1. What's Charles Knapp's e-mail address? (Hint: he works at the University of Georgia.)

2. What's the U.S. President's e-mail address?

3. Does your organization have a phone book? If so, check your personal details.

Usenet News

Usenet News is a vast set of discussion lists on a wide range of topics. **Newsgroups** are organized in a tree structure of discussion topics. While the number of top level categories varies with the news server to which you gain access, eight common major categories are shown in Table 5-3. A complete list of newsgroups is available.[7] Client programs, generally known as newsreaders, are available to access a news server. You run a special program to read the news, and you must have access to a news server.

Usenet is based on a series of news servers that transfer messages to each other so that all postings to a newsgroup are replicated on all news servers. When a message is posted to a newsgroup on a particular server, it passes the message on to any news servers to which it talks. In this way, a message posted on one server eventually appears on all other servers.

The Web offers several ways of accessing newsgroups. The simplest approach is to click on Netscape's Newsgroups button (see Figure 5-7), part of the directory strip discussed in the first section of this chapter.

---

6. http://www.uga.edu/
7. http://www.ph.tn.tudelft.nl/People/pierre/anchorman/Amn.html

Table 5-3: Common major news categories

Category	Description
alt	Alternative—just about anything that's not mainstream
comp	Computer science, software sources, and information on hardware and software systems (e.g., comp.databases)
misc	Topics not covered by the other categories (e.g., misc.forsale)
news	News network maintenance, and software (e.g., news.admin.policy)
rec	Hobbies and recreation (e.g., rec.arts.cinema)
sci	Sciences (e.g., sci.astro.hubble)
soc	Social issues and social communications (e.g., soc.culture.australia)
talk	Discussion and debate on a variety of subjects (e.g., talk.politics.gun)

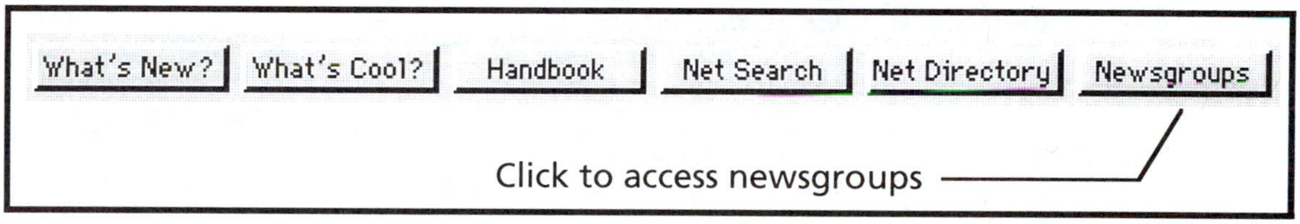

Figure 5-7. Netscape's support for Newsgroups

You can also access a newsgroup by typing its URL in the location box and pressing Enter (see Figure 5-8)

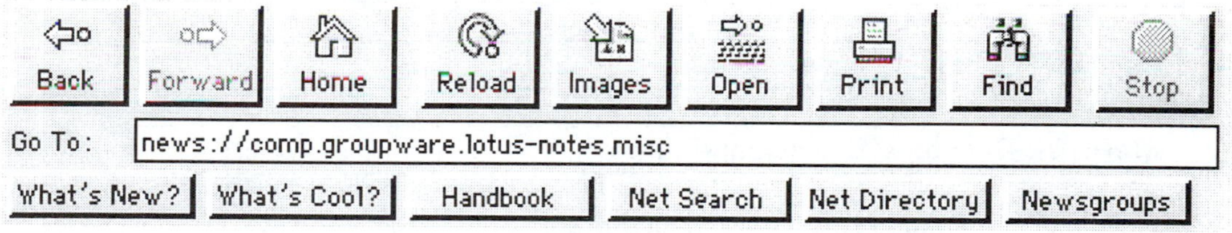

Figure 5-8. Accessing a newsgroup using the location window

You can create a link to any newsgroup by specifying its URL within a HTML statement. The HTML in Table 5-4 illustrates how you define the link to the Lotus Notes discussion group, a useful discussion group for Lotus Notes' developers. Notice that the link does not indicate the address of the news server because you probably will always access the same news server. Thus, you specify your local news server in your preference settings[8] (see Figure 5-9). In our case, the news reader is news.uga.edu.

---

8. The first entry under Netscape's Options menu.

Table 5-4: Usenet News in HTML

Server	Browser
`<a href = "news://comp.groupware.lo-tus-notes.misc" Lotus Notes news</a>`	Lotus Notes news

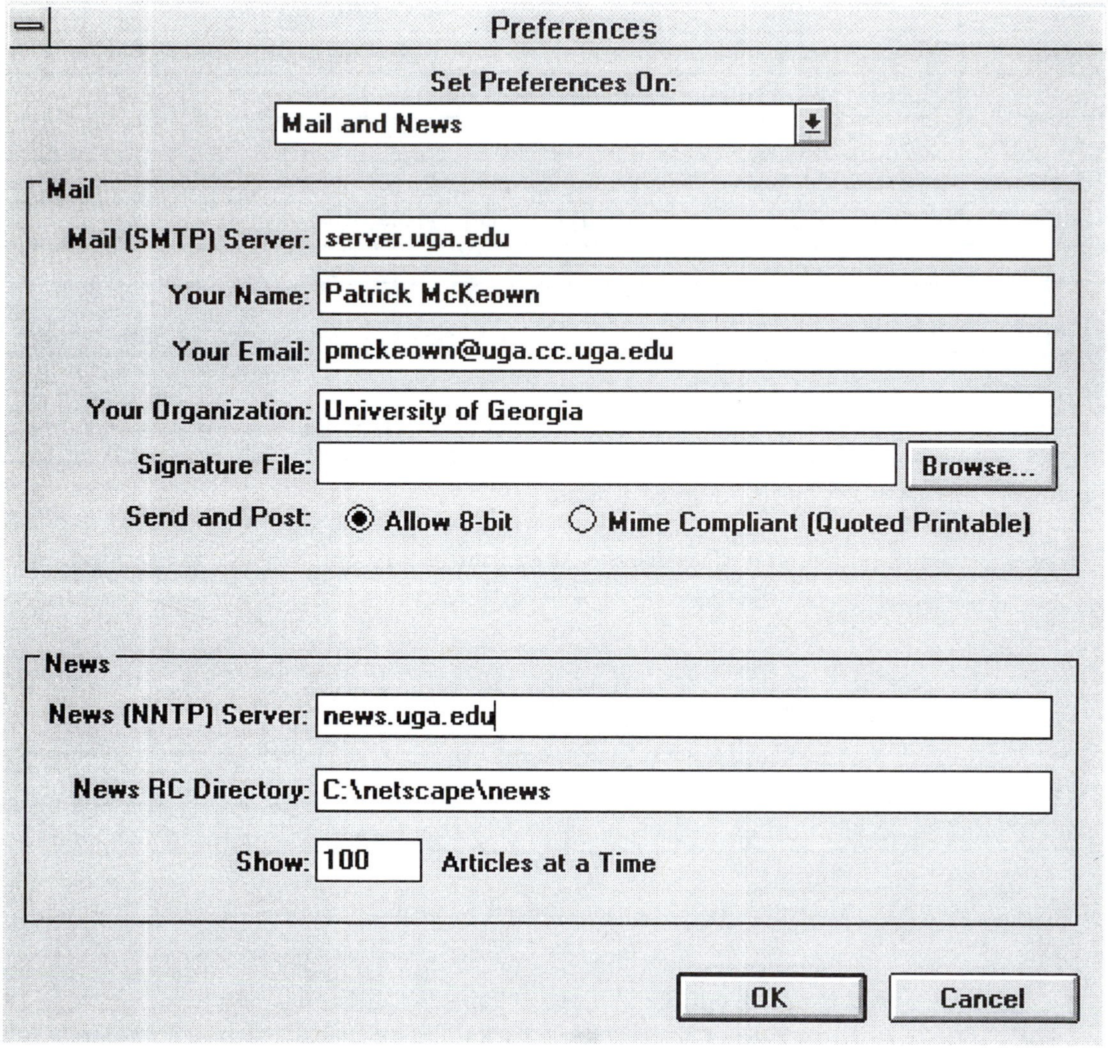

Figure 5-9. Mail and News preferences

1. What are the current hot topics for rec.backcountry?
2. ClariNet Communications Corp. publishes the ClariNet e.News, which appears as a major news category for many news readers. Check out whether your organization subscribes to the clari newsgroup. If so, read the latest news from Australia (clari.world.oceania.australia).
3. What is the address of the news reader for your organization? Is its address set for your browser?
4. Is there a newsgroup for Internet topics? What is it called? What topics are discussed by the members of this group?

Discussion lists

Discussion lists, another common use of the Internet, are built on e-mail facilities. An electronic meeting can easily be established for people with a common interest. Information exchange is facilitated by setting up an e-mail address to which any member of the group can send a message. The software then automatically distributes the message to everyone on the list.

There are thousands of mailing lists. Some are very active with lots of traffic and others are dormant. A list of publicly available mailing lists is maintained on the Web.[9] You can join any of them. There are also many private lists for which membership is controlled. For example, a firm may want to maintain a restricted list for communication with its major customers.

Be careful when replying to a message sent to a mailing list. The default is often to send a message to all subscribers, not just the person who originated the message. Failure to remember this procedure has frequently resulted in the embarrassment of a few and the amusement of many.

Your turn!

1. What is the major difference between a discussion list and a newsgroup?
2. Subscribe to a discussion list that you fancy and report what happens.

---

9. http://www.NeoSoft.com/internet/paml/

> **FAQs and TV trivia**
>
> Obscure details of hundreds of TV shows are now available as FAQs. TV net (HTTP://www.tvnet.com) has about 13,000 links to more than 400 current and past TV shows. Most of the sites are run by fans.
>
> From the FAQs for the newsgroup for the Simpsons (alt.tv.simpsons), you can discover:
>
> What the "J" stands for in Homer J. and Bart J. Simpson?
>
> Which one's Itchy and which one's Scratchy?
>
> If you are a fan of Seinfeld, check newsgroup alt.tv.seinfeld and find the answer to the following questions:
>
> What is Kramer's full name?
>
> Where is the diner?
>
> Adapted from: L. Miller, Internet fun FAQs catch you up on TV trivia. *USA Today.* September 7, 1995; D6.

FTP

FTP (File Transfer Protocol) supports high speed file transfer over the Internet. To make it easy to find the files you might want to copy, FTP also permits listing of directories. To transfer files, you generally need permission to access the host machine; however, because in many cases seeking approval would be burdensome and defeat the information sharing goal of the Internet, **anonymous FTP** is available, which opens a portion of a host's file space to all comers. Files are publicly available and may be copied. Many of the thousands of anonymous FTP hosts contain free software, shareware, and software upgrades.[10] Some useful anonymous FTP sites are shown in Table 5-5.

Table 5-5: Some anonymous FTP sites

Server	Company
ftp.microsoft.com	Microsoft
ftp.apple.com	Apple
ftp.adobe.com	Adobe

Web browsers provide FTP support via the location window and HTML. The FTP address of a file or directory can be entered in the location window, as shown in Figure 5-10, where the main directory for Microsoft's anonymous FTP site is displayed.

An anonymous FTP file can be retrieved from within a Web application by using a URL of the form (see also the example shown in Table 5-6)

---

10. Check out http://ici.proper.com/1/pc/files

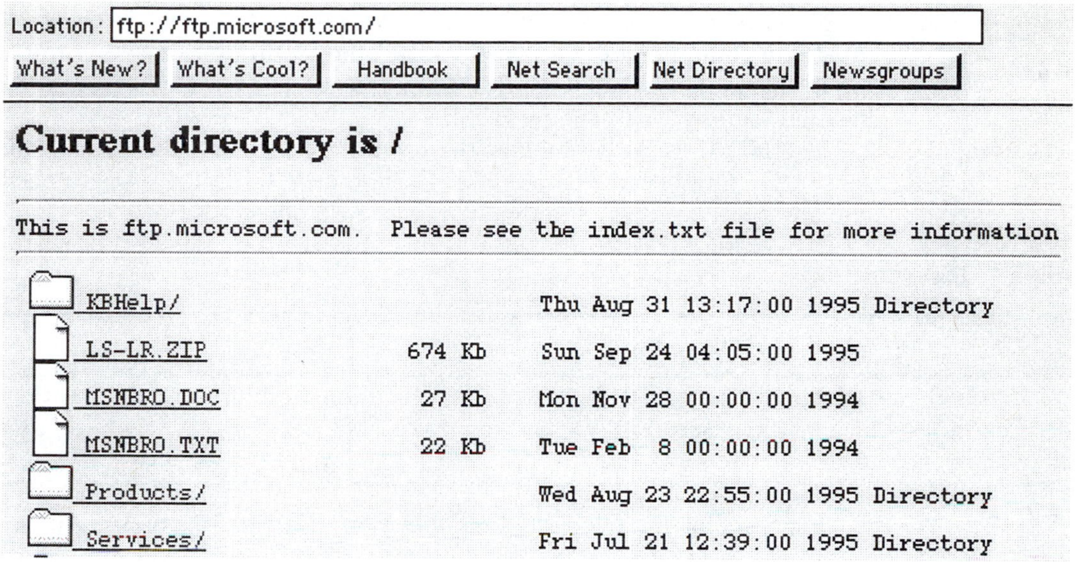

```
Location: ftp://ftp.microsoft.com/
```
```
What's New?   What's Cool?   Handbook   Net Search   Net Directory   Newsgroups
```

Current directory is /

This is ftp.microsoft.com. Please see the index.txt file for more information

📁 KBHelp/		Thu Aug 31 13:17:00 1995 Directory
📄 LS-LR.ZIP	674 Kb	Sun Sep 24 04:05:00 1995
📄 MSNBRO.DOC	27 Kb	Mon Nov 28 00:00:00 1994
📄 MSNBRO.TXT	22 Kb	Tue Feb 8 00:00:00 1994
📁 Products/		Wed Aug 23 22:55:00 1995 Directory
📁 Services/		Fri Jul 21 12:39:00 1995 Directory

Figure 5-10. Accessing FTP using the location window

```
ftp://computer address:port/path
```

For example, Dell uses FTP to distribute press releases. The URL for downloading a press release issued on May 9th, 1995 is:

```
ftp://dell1.us.dell.com/dellbbs/info/950509.txt
```

If you specify a directory instead of a file, most browsers will give you a list of the directory's contents and allow you to select files or other directories. For example, to see all of the available Dell press releases, use:

```
ftp://dell1.us.dell.com/dellbbs/info/
```

Table 5-6: FTP in HTML

Server	Browser
`<a href="ftp://ftp.negia.net/webbook/put-down.txt> Great putdowns"></a>`	<u>Great putdowns</u>

■ ■ — ■ — ■ — ■ — ■ — ■ — ■ — ■ — ■ — ■ — ■

Your turn!

1. Use the location window of your browser to access the FTP site for this book (ftp.negia.net/webbook) and retrieve putdown.txt.

2. Write HTML to provide FTP access to a Dell press release.

3. Why is anonymous FTP useful?

Telnet

Telnet is the main Internet protocol for connecting to a remote machine. It enables you to work on another computer on the Internet. Of course, you must have an authorized account on the other computer or be permitted to log in as an anonymous or general user. You can use telnet via the browser's location window or by coding HTML.

The HTML is fairly obvious, the service is *telnet*, and the address of the computer and port are specified. There is no need to indicate a path because you are trying to access a computer, not locate a file (see Table 5-7).

Table 5-7: Telnet in HTML

Server	Browser
`<a href = "telnet: //martini.eecs.umich.edu:3000/"> Geographic database server</a>`	Geographic database server

Incidentally, the telnet command shown in Table 5-7 connects you to a database listing information for cities in the United States and some international locations. The database is searchable by city name, zip code, etc., and reports data such as county, state, latitude and longitude, population, elevation, and zip code(s). Entering Athens, GA yields the output of Figure 5-11.

```
0 Athens
1 13059 Clarke
2 GA Georgia
3 US United States
R county seat
F 45 Populated place
L 33 57 39 N 83 22 41 W
P 42549
E 662
Z 30601 30602 30603 30604 30605 30606 30607 30609 30610 30612
```

Figure 5-11. Output from the geographic database server

Your turn!

1. Using your Web browser, telnet to the geographic database and report the location of U.S. cities called Oslo. Also find Hell.
2. Check out whether you can telnet to your college or university's library and, if possible, do so.

Gopher

A distributed document search and retrieval system created prior to the Web, **Gopher** is another Internet tool. Developed at the University of Minnesota, whose mascot is a gopher, this tool helps you find information stored on Gopher servers. Lacking hypertext and integrated multimedia support, Gopher has been substantially replaced by the Web. Many organizations have ceased development of Gopher applications in favor of the Web. In addition, they have linked their Web applications to their residual Gopher documents. Thus, the Web has become a common interface to Gopher.

A Gopher client has a complete view of all Gopher information, even though it is on many different servers. The beauty of Gopher is its transparency; the client is not concerned with the location of a Gopher server. The main navigation aid is a hierarchical menu. The top level menu guides you to data sources at your server and provides connections to other Gopher servers. To gain some idea of the variety of information available, check out Gopher Jewels.[11]

Gopher servers can be accessed using URLs in a manner similar to HTTP servers. The major difference is in the file specification: Gopher protocol requires a numeric code to specify the type of file. These codes are specified in the path name, preceding the name of the file being accessed. Most of the time, you will use a code of 1 because you will first open the directory.

One way to access Gopher is to enter the URL in the location window of the browser (see Figure 5-12). Notice that the URL indicates the port (70) to be used and that a directory (code = 1) is to be retrieved. In this case, if you omit both the port number and directory code (i.e., use gopher://gopher.uga.edu), the request is still successful.

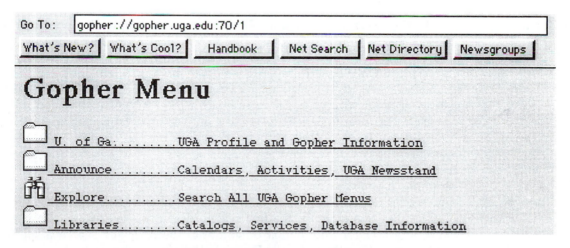

Figure 5-12. Accessing Gopher using the location window

Consider the situation of a manufacturer who does considerable business with Israel. Because of the volatility of the region, the firm wants to remain

---

11. http://galaxy.einet.net/GJ/index.html

vigilant regarding opportunities and threats to its business. Consequently, it wants to maintain a link from its internal information system to the Israel Information Service. The URL in Table 5-8 illustrates how the firm can establish a link from its Web page to the Israel Information Service's directory. Clicking on the link opens the Gopher directory.

Table 5-8: Gopher URL example

Server	Browser

`<a href=gopher:`
`//israel-info.gov.il:70/1>`
`The Israel Information Service</a>`
	The Israel Information Service

Your turn!

1. Access the Israel Information Service and report the type of information it provides.

2. Access the Gopher server at the University of Alaska (gopher://info.alaska.edu:70/1) and report the current Anchorage weather.

3. Visit The University of Georgia's Gopher server and report the start and end dates for the next quarter.

WAIS

WAIS (Wide Area Information Servers), a project originally sponsored by Dow Jones & Co., Apple Computer, KPMG Peat Marwick, and Thinking Machines Corporation, became WAIS Inc.,[12] which was recently purchased by America Online. WAIS supports access to a wide variety of electronically published material—books, magazines, news information, product data sheets, technical overviews, company information, encyclopedias, and more. It also facilitates automatic indexing and publishing of large databases.

You can try out WAIS through WAISGATE[13] (see Figure 5-13). WAIS searching is a two-stage process. First, you need to access the directory of servers to identify a database that should contain details of the topic. For example, if you were interested in finding out more about French Polynesia, you would used the keyword *country* to find a server that contains details of nations. For this example, the first search identifies *The World Factbook* as a suitable server for information on countries. Second, you search a specific server for pertinent details (e.g., French Polynesia in our example).

An interesting and very useful feature of WAIS is that a user can indicate which retrieved documents are relevant to the current search, and then re-run

---

12. http://www.wais.com:80/

13. http://www.wais.com:80/newhomepages/search.html

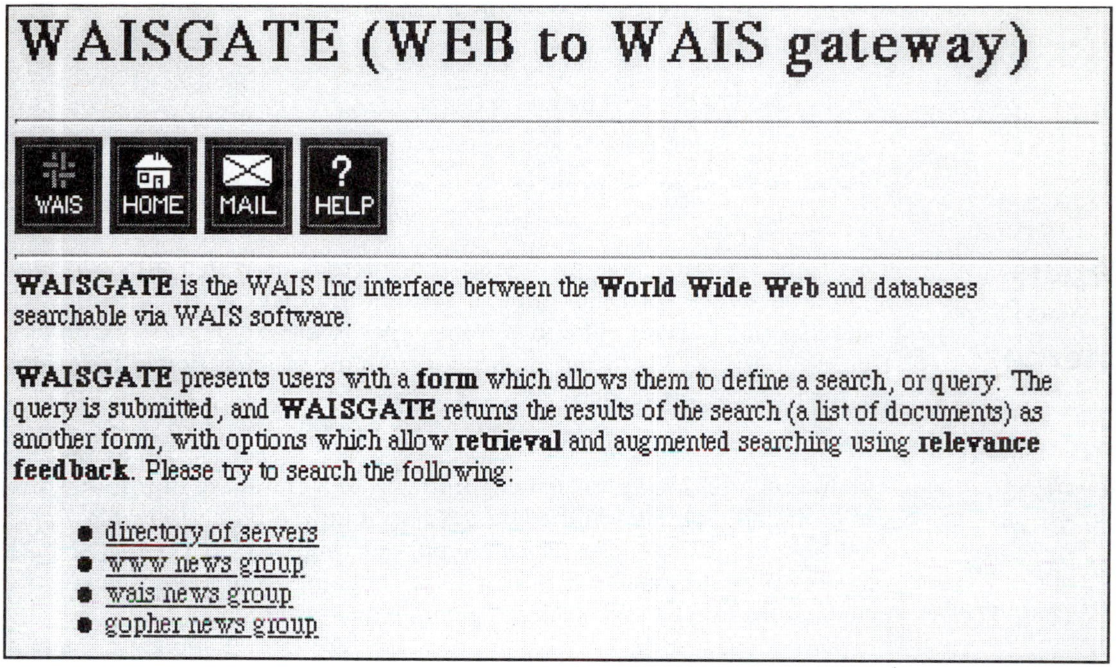

Figure 5-13. Web to WAIS gateway

the search. The server attempts to find documents similar to those marked as relevant. In the present WAIS system, similar documents are simply ones which share a large number of common words. This method of information retrieval is called *relevance feedback*.

Compared to most of the Web search engines, WAIS is possibly more precise because you limit searching to specific servers, whereas most Web search facilities search all Web pages or links. As you soon discover, a Web search can retrieve many links that have little apparent relationship to the key words of the search.

WAIS and Web searching have some similarities and differences. Conceptually, both are similar in that they form an index of the words in each document (ignoring words such as *a* and *the*), which is used subsequently when searching. Documents containing a relatively high frequency of the sought word or words are reported by the search. WAIS is more deliberate in its approach because when documents are stored on a WAIS server, they are automatically indexed. Web search engines rely on two less rigorous approaches to indexing because search engines and Web documents are usually on different servers. First, a document can be voluntarily registered with a search engine, as discussed previously. Second, a program can prowl the Web to find the documents at each Web site and index them. Another important difference is that WAIS searches documents on WAIS servers, and Web searching scans documents on Web servers.

Your turn!

1. Use WAIS to get details of Nepal.
2. How could your organization use WAIS?

Popular uses of the Internet

There are several common uses of the Internet of which all new surfers should be aware. MUDs (a popular form of Internet entertainment), Project Gutenberg (conversion of books from paper to electronic format), and electronic publishing, a growing application with the proliferation of the Internet, are the focus of this section.

MUDs— a frontier for exploration

The Internet does have an element of fun. **MUDs** (multiple user dungeons or dimensions) originated in the late 1980s as multiple-user, electronic versions of the game "Dungeons and Dragons." A virtual world populated by the players and their creations, a MUD is an ongoing drama with an electronically assembled cast exploring and interacting in cyberspace.[14]

Particularly addictive for students, MUDs were banned in Australia because their introduction sparked a 25 percent increase in Internet traffic out of the country. Some universities have banned MUDs because they waste too many computing resources and student time. You have been warned! Be wary of MUDs consuming your time. As you would expect, a list of MUD home pages is on the Web.[15]

Today's MUDs may be prototypical of virtual worlds that will appear in the future. These worlds will move beyond the constrained text interchange of present MUDs to become multimedia. They may also become vehicles for social interaction. A MUD could be an ideal way for an organization to develop team spirit in a group that never meets face-to-face. Teams need play time if they are to develop the social bonding that is a precursor to goal commitment and successful project implementation. Many teams develop their social dimension outside of formal work assignments. For example, a team might lunch together after a meeting. Virtual teams, those formed by electronic links, need to find ways to socialize, and a MUD might be a convenient way of electronically developing a cohesive team.[16]

---

14. This term was coined by William Gibson in his 1984 novel *Neuromancer*.

15. http://www.cis.upenn.edu:80/~lwl/mhome.html

16. For expanded discussion of MUDs and their organizational application see M. O. Devereaux and R. Johansen. *Bridging distance and diversity: navigating the challenges of distributed and cross-cultural business teams.* Menlo Park, CA: The Institute for the Future, 1993.

■ ■

Your turn!

1. Who is in charge of the Envy MUD? (Hint: check out the Web site describing MUDs.)

■ ■

Project Gutenberg

The world has accumulated a vast collection of knowledge and literature in printed form. To gain full benefit of these prior achievements, a number of projects are underway to place these works on the Internet. Project Gutenberg,[17] perhaps one of the most well-known of these endeavors, is converting printed text to electronic format for selected works. Generally, these are well-known books for which the copyright has expired or copyrighted books for which electronic distribution has been approved. Some of the books available include *Alice's Adventures in Wonderland* by Lewis Carroll, *The Red Badge of Courage* by Stephen Crane, and *The Autobiography of Ben Franklin* by Benjamin Franklin.

Project Gutenberg asserts that it produces about one million dollars for each hour of its work. This claim is based on an estimate of one hundred hours to take a text, check its copyright, and convert it to electronic format. Project Gutenberg then projects its potential audience at one hundred million readers and gives each electronic text a nominal value of one dollar. The long-term goal of Project Gutenberg is to give away one trillion (10^9) electronic books by 2001.

There are several projects to create electronic texts, and some people are managing projects for particular authors or characters. For example, the Sherlock Holmes site[18] is a collection of electronic texts, facts, and minutiae of Arthur Conan Doyle's famous detective.

■ ■

Your turn!

1. Why aren't all of the Sherlock Holmes' stories available electronically? Find out by visiting the appropriate home page.

■ ■

Electronic exchange of documents

The development of the Internet has created two important opportunities. First, people working in different parts of the world and for different organizations can just as readily collaborate as two people in the same firm working in adjacent offices. Second, anyone who has access to a Web server can become a publisher. Those with Web access can make their writings available

---

17. http://jg.cso.uiuc.edu/pg/pg_home.html
18. http://watserv1.uwaterloo.ca/~credmond/sh.html

to the world. Exploitation of these opportunities requires the capacity to share documents. At the simplest level, sharing can be done through simple text files; however, text files are a very inelegant solution because they are unformatted and do not support the exchange of graphics. Ideally, the reader of a shared document should see exactly the same image as the creator. There are two approaches to maintaining the image fidelity of the original document.

First, the author and the reader can synchronize their software. Both could agree to use the same word processor and, in some cases, to agree to use the same operating system. Then files can be exchanged using FTP or as encoded (e.g., binhex or uuencode[19]) attachments to e-mail messages. This approach is particularly useful for joint authorship of articles because all parties can read and amend the work. Forcing people to adopt the same word processor is not necessary, however, if the main goal is to share documents.

The second approach is to use a common format for **electronic documents**. Ideally, what you would like to do is create an electronic copy of a printed document and share it. Now, thanks to several available products, this is possible. Using Adobe's Acrobat Exchange, any document created by a DOS, Macintosh, Windows, or UNIX application can be converted to Adobe's **Portable Document Format (PDF)**. Producing a PDF document is very similar to printing, except the image is sent to a file instead of a printer. The fidelity of the original document is maintained—text, graphics, and tables are faithfully reproduced when the PDF file is printed or viewed.

PDF has been adopted by a number of organizations., including the Internal Revenue Service[20] for tax forms and *The New York Times*[21] for an eight-page summary of its newspaper. PDF documents can be sent as e-mail attachments, retrieved using FTP, or accessed from a Web application. To decipher a PDF file the recipient must use a special reader, supplied at no cost by Adobe[22] for all major operating systems. In the case of the Web, you have to configure your browser to invoke the Adobe Acrobat reader whenever a file with the extension pdf is retrieved.

Your turn!

1. Search the Web for some useful or interesting applications of Adobe's Acrobat Exchange. Where would be a good place to start looking?

2. Describe some potential applications of electronic publishing.

3. Discuss the pros and cons of electronic versus paper publication.

---

19. Methods for converting non-text files (non-ASCII) into ASCII because Internet e-mail can handle only ASCII.

20. http://www.ustreas.gov/treasury/bureaus/irs/taxforms.html

21. http://nytimesfax.com/

22. http://www.adobe.com:80/Acrobat/Acrobat0.html

> **A very personal experience**
>
> We wrote this book using different word processors (WordPerfect and Microsoft Word) on different platforms (Windows and Macintosh). A final camera ready version was created using FrameMaker on a Macintosh PowerPC. We exchanged files using FTP.
>
> The process was not completely seamless. For example, Word-Perfect on Windows could not successfully translate Microsoft Word for the Mac files. Thus, we had to first convert Macintosh Word files to Windows Word files and then to WordPerfect format.
>
> Why didn't we standardize on the same word processor and operating system? Because one of us is a Mac fanatic and the other a recalcitrant Windows WordPerfect user.
>
> Why did we change to FrameMaker instead of using Word or WordPerfect for the camera-ready version? Because we found we needed the full functionality of document publishing software to manage the placement of tables and figures.

Encryption and signing

Societies have always needed secure methods of transmitting highly sensitive information and confirming the identity of the sender. Coding or encryption techniques, as old as writing, have been used for thousands of years to maintain the confidentiality of messages. In an earlier time, messages were sealed with the sender's personal signet ring—a simple, but easily forged, method of authentication. We still rely on personal signatures for checks and legal contracts, but how do you sign an e-mail message? In the information age, we need electronic encryption and signing for the orderly conduct of business, government, and personal correspondence.

Internet messages can pass through many computers on their way from sender to receiver, and there is always the danger that a *sniffer* program on an intermediate computer briefly intercepts and reads a message. In most cases, this will not cause you great concern, but what happens if your message contains your name, credit card number, and expiry date? The sniffer program, looking for a typical credit card number of the form nnnn nnnn nnnn nnnn (where n is a digit), copies your message before letting it continue its normal progress. Now, the owner of the rogue program can use your credit card details to purchase products in your name and charge them to your account.

Without a secure means of transmitting payment information, customers and merchants will be very reluctant to place and receive orders, respectively. When the customer places an order, the Web browser should automatically encrypt the order prior to transmission—this is not the customer's task.

Credit card numbers are not the only sensitive information transmitted on the Internet. Because it is a general transport system for electronic information, the Internet can carry a wide range of confidential information (financial reports, sales figures, marketing strategies, technology reports, and so on). If senders and receivers cannot be sure that their communication is strictly private, they will not use the Internet. Secure transmission of information is necessary for electronic commerce to thrive.

Encryption

Encryption is the process of transforming messages or data to protect their meaning. Encryption scrambles a message so that it is meaningful only to the person knowing the method of encryption and the key to deciphering it. To everybody else, it is gobbledygook. The reverse process, **decryption**, converts a seemingly senseless character string into the original message. A popular form of encryption, readily available to Internet users, goes by the name of Pretty Good Privacy (PGP) and is distributed on the Web.[23] PGP is a public domain implementation of **public-key** encryption.

Traditional encryption, which uses the same key to encode and decode a message, has a very significant problem. How do you securely distribute the key? It can't be sent with the message because if the message is intercepted, the key can be used to decipher it. You must find another secure medium for transmitting the key. So, do you fax the key or phone it? Either method is not completely secure and is time consuming whenever the key is changed. Also, how do you know that the key's receiver will protect its secrecy?

A public-key encryption system has two keys: one private and the other public. A public key can be freely distributed because it is quite separate from its corresponding **private key**. To send and receive messages, communicators first need to create separate pairs of private and public keys and then exchange their public keys. The sender encrypts a message with the intended receiver's public key, and upon receiving the message, the receiver applies her private key (see Figure 5-14). The receiver's private key, the only one that can decrypt the message, must be kept secret to permit secure message exchange.

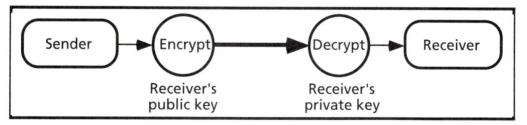

Figure 5-14. Encryption with a public key system

The elegance of the public-key system is that it totally avoids the problem of secure transmission of keys. Public keys can be freely exchanged. Indeed, there can be a public database containing each person's or organization's public key. For instance, if you want to e-mail your credit card details to a catalog company, you can simply obtain its public key (probably from its Web site) and encrypt your entire message prior to transmission. Of course, you may wish to transmit far more important data than your credit card number.

---

23. http://web.mit.edu/network/pgp

```
        To:  Pat McKeown <pmckeown@cbacc.cba.uga.edu>
      From:  rwatson@uga.cc.uga.edu (Rick Watson)
   Subject:  Money
        Cc:
       Bcc:
Attachments:
```
G'day Pat
I hope you are enjoying your stay in Switzerland.

Could you do me a favor? I need $50,000 from my secret Swiss bank account. The name of the bank is Aussie-Swiss International in Geneva. The account code is 451-3329 and the password is 'meekatharra'

I'll see you (and the money) at the airport this Friday.

Cheers

Rick

Figure 5-15. Message before encryption

Consider the message shown in Figure 5-15; the sender would hardly want this message to fall into the wrong hands. After encryption with PGP, the message is totally secure (see Figure 5-16). Only the receiver, using his private key, can decode the message.

```
        To:  Pat McKeown <pmckeown@cbacc.cba.uga.edu>
      From:  rwatson@uga.cc.uga.edu (Rick Watson)
   Subject:  Money
        Cc:
       Bcc:
Attachments:
```

```
-----BEGIN PGP MESSAGE-----
Version: 2.6.2

hEwDfOTG8eEvuiEBAf9I5A8zgwZukkn2j7tbH8U/7692yeOffOQIPh00eX/4mNYg
HYp2HepBy9OssueWjNk1plq11oxYkw3jPSsc/YCDpgAAAQvUm+SN6KnEFAHCFd2
dp9X3o3Z3gDjx2SriX1lutgVqFaiD4ltklOlp9H5YQr6VkpavvdygGTdpdQB7gXA
Zttxy4j0hujbpAQCbUY8hNmDimRk\vhI1Ejmksebnmmq Lc9bcRfLy/N0L9B3GqjgJ
rl83reSiQLxwRxb72LnvgCdDlr0P9dzUs5PYexnIT8O+Ui2ENMCdc/fSSwGexVYZ
np5rBtQ5p2wrzkfEeLHFQSv7iTjTVQRGsXjFB38ZlksaES7+WvvMOx\v666fzBP2HC
JVI7IfQNXB9vfq8s8WfB1AHmEPbuyOdf5rvPzQJ1zhMex5fDK4HcuAe3Z/E0fhqU
7enHiQvwxCgYZPKNGto=
=RSca
-----END PGP MESSAGE-----
```

Figure 5-16. Message after encryption

Signing   In addition, a public-key encryption system can be used to authenticate messages In cases where the content of the message is not confidential, the receiver may still wish to verify the sender's identity. For example, one of your friends may find it amusing to have some fun at your expense (see Figure 5-17).

```
        To:  Richard T. Watson <rwatson@uga.cc.uga.edu>
      From:  President@whitehouse.gov
   Subject:  Invitation to visit the White House
        Cc:
       Bcc:
Attachments:
```
....
Dear Dr. Watson
It is my pleasure to invite you to a special meeting of Internet users at the White House on April 1st at 2pm. Please call 212-123-7890 and ask for Mr. A. Phool for complete details of your visit.

The President

Figure 5-17. Message before signing

If the President indeed was in the habit of communicating electronically, it is likely that he would sign his messages so that the receiver could verify it. A sender's private key is used to created **a signed message**. The receiver then applies the sender's public key to verify the signature (see Figure 5-18).

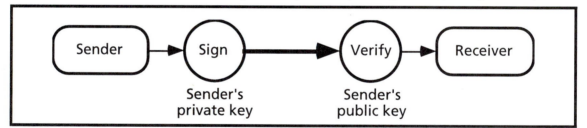

Figure 5-18. Signing with a public key system

A signed message has additional encrypted text containing the sender's signature (see Figure 5-19). When the purported sender's public key is applied to this message, the identity of the sender can be verified (it was not the President).

Imagine you pay $1,000 per year for an investment information service. The provider might want to verify that any e-mail requests it receives are from subscribers. Thus, as part of the subscription sign-up, subscribers have to supply their public key, and when using the service, sign all electronic messages with their private key. The provider is then assured that it is servicing paying customers. Naturally, any messages between the service and the client should be encrypted to ensure that others do not gain from the information.

```
        To:  Richard T. Watson <rwatson@uga.cc.uga.edu>
      From:  President@whitehouse.gov
   Subject:  Invitation to visit the White House
        Cc:
       Bcc:
Attachments:
...............................................................................
Dear Dr. Watson
It is my pleasure to invite you to a special meeting of Internet users at the White House on April
1st at 2pm. Please call 212-123-7890 and ask for Mr. A. Phool for complete details of your visit.

The President

-----BEGIN PGP SIGNATURE----
Version: 2.6.2

iQBVAwUBMGXuWHzkovHhL7ohAQFqbAIAs292DJuclogmEkkkJkAuMu8+5+qrMdyt
dCDDBvILp\8ornqKqkFVypgT1DUpebbeY8x9EAakhCEPUuelQuXKcVQ==
=T7mg
-----END PGP SIGNATURE----
```

Figure 5-19. Message after signing

Key terms and con-cepts	decryption	PDF
	discussion list	phonebook
	e-mail	private key
	electronic document	public key
	encryption	signing
	FTP	Telnet
	Gopher	Usenet News
	listserver	WAIS
	MUD	web directory
	newsgroups	web searching

- - - - - - - - - - - - - - -

Exercises

1. What's the difference between encryption and signing?
2. What is the advantage of a public-key encryption system?
3. When would you use both encryption and signing.
4. We did not discuss Archie and Veronica. Use the Web to discover how Archie is connected to FTP and Veronica to Gopher.

- - - - - - - - - - - - - - -

6   Business and the Internet

∎ ∎

Objectives

After completing this chapter, you will be able to:

❖ explain why an organization should consider using the Web;

❖ identify organizations that should be using the Web;

❖ identify opportunities for organizations to use the Web.

Introduction

The previous chapters have laid the foundation for understanding how to use the Web, write Web applications, and use other Internet tools. Now it is time to learn how to exploit the Internet, and the Web in particular, to improve organizational performance. In the introduction to the first chapter, we argued that organizations need to make a metamorphosis—they have to abandon existing business practices to create new ways of interacting with stakeholders. This chapter will provide you with the insights to understand how an organization can make the transformation from caterpillar to butterfly.

While we can emphatically assert that organizations need to make a metamorphosis, but how do they begin? The problem is that there are few guidelines for identifying who should use the Web and how it can be used. This chapter presents useful frameworks and examples for stimulating thinking about possible applications. Frameworks provide a structure to aid systematic consideration of opportunities. Examples foster analogical thinking—"We have a situation similar to that example. With a few modifications and twists, we could do the same."

Why use the Web?

Every business faces three strategic challenges: demand risk, innovation risk, and inefficiency risk.[1] The Internet, and the Web in particular, can be a device for reducing these risks.

Demand risk

Sharply changing demand or the collapse of markets poses a significant risk for many firms. Smith-Corona (as mentioned in Chapter 1), one of the last U.S. manufacturers of typewriters, recently filed for bankruptcy. Cheap personal computers have destroyed the typewriter market. In simple terms, **demand risk** means fewer customers want to buy a firm's wares. The globalization of the world market and increasing deregulation expose firms to greater levels of competition and magnify the threat of demand risk. To counter it, firms need to be flexible, adaptive, and continually searching for new markets and stimulating demand for their products and services.

The Web is global; millions of people have Web access, and this number is growing rapidly. Furthermore, many Web users are well-educated, affluent consumers—an ideal target for consumer marketing. Any firm establishing a Web presence, no matter how small or localized, instantly enters global marketing. The firm's message can be read by anyone with Web access. The South African[2] wine retailer, introduced in Chapter 1, can market to the entire Web world with a few pages on the Web. The economies of scale and scope enjoyed by large organizations are considerably diminished. Small producers do not have to negotiate the business practices of foreign climes in order to expose their products to new markets. They can safely venture forth electronically from their home base. Fortunately, the infrastructure—international credit cards (e.g., Visa) and international delivery systems (e.g., FedEx)—for global marketing already exists. Add Web advertising and global marketing becomes a reality for many firms wherever they are located. Thus, the Web offers an excellent opportunity for reducing demand risk by diversifying into new markets.

A new medium for advertising, the Web enables firms to develop a home page where their products and services are described and promoted in considerable detail. Thousands of companies now have a Web presence and in the foreseeable future nearly every company, from Fortune 500 giants, such as General Motors,[3] to small organizations such as Carroll EMC,[4] will be on the Web because it is a cheap and effective means of informing customers. For instance, for as little as $50 per month, a company can promote its wares on a commercial Web server.

A particular advantage of Web advertising is that it can be changed very quickly. Advertisements for traditional media—print, radio, and TV—are not as fortunate. For example, a glossy brochure may take weeks to prepare and

---

1. J. Child, Information technology, organizations, and the response to strategic challenges. *California Management Review.* Fall 1987: 33-50.

2. http://www.os2.iaccess.za/index.html

3. http://www.yahoo.com/Entertainment/Automobiles/General_Motors/

4. http://www.southwire.com/wgta/mempages/cemc/cemcover.htm

distribute, and there is still the danger that many customers are referring to an older version. A Web home page can be updated easily and quickly and customers always see the latest version. Web advertising means firms can react quickly to changing demand and adjust customer communication with alacrity.

Alternatively, firms can advertise on the Web. For example, EDS has an advertisement on the *What's New?* page of Netscape.[5] Because many people visit this Netscape page, the EDS message is highly visible. This form of advertising is very similar to using a billboard on a busy highway. The key to Web advertising, like most advertising, is to make the message visible to customers who are most likely to purchase. Thus, fast food outlets advertise on interstate highways because many passing customers need to stop for a meal. Similarly, firms who advertise on the Web must be certain that the *passing traffic* is likely to be interested in what they have to offer, otherwise the message is wasted and, even worse, irritating to possible customers. In most cases, Web advertising is simply a link, usually in the form of the company's logo, to a home page.

Table 6-1: Marketing strategies

Traditional marketing	Web marketing
Mass marketing	Customer convergence
Market segmentation	
One-to-one marketing	

Traditional advertising has progressed through three stages (see Figure 6-1). Initially, **mass marketing** simply broadcast the same message to all customers. For many, this message was irrelevant because they were not interested in the product, or inappropriate because they were interested in a different form of the product. For instance, the customer seeking a luxury car finds an advertisement for a compact car inappropriate. Consequently, advertisers adopted **market segmentation**, and targeted their communication by addressing particular messages to segments of the market. For example, the advertisement for the luxury car appears in *The Wall Street Journal* and the compact car ad is displayed in a campus newspaper. More recently, because firms have been amassing vast collections of data about their customers, they can direct specific messages to particular customers—so called **one-to-one marketing**.[6] The buying pattern of a customer who regularly purchases jazz CDs at a music store chain, for example, could be identified by that chain's database system. As a result, the customer may receive regular mailings describing new jazz releases, perhaps with a coupon for a 10 percent discount. Web advertising reverses the flow of communication. Instead of send-

---

5. http://home.netscape.com/home/whats-new.html

6. D. Peppers and M. Rogers, *The one to one future: building relationships one customer at a time.* New York: Currency Doubleday, 1993.

ing messages to customers, the firm now wants customers to converge on its home page. **Customer convergence** is the key to Web marketing. Unless customers find a firm's home page, the entire effort is wasted. This means a firm must ensure that its home page is found by any of the search engines a customer may elect to use. Even more, a firm with many products must ensure that potential customers converge on the page that describes the product or service of greatest potential interest. Thus, a camera manufacturer must first make certain that photography enthusiasts find its home page, and then help the potential customer, possibly with the aid of an expert system, navigate to the pages describing cameras or lenses of interest.

Innovation risk

Failure to be as innovative as competitors—**innovation risk**—is a second challenge. In an era of accelerating technological development, the firm that fails to continually improve its products and services is likely to lose market share to competitors and maybe even disappear. To remain alert to potential innovations, among other things, firms need an open flow of concepts and ideas. Customers are one particular source of innovative ideas because they adapt and redesign products and services to meet their evolving needs. Thus, firms need to find efficient and effective means of continual communication with customers.

Internet communication (e-mail, lists, and Usenet news) can be used to create open communication links with a wide range of customers. E-mail can facilitate frequent communication with the most innovative customers. A list can be created to enable any customer to request product changes or new features. The advantage of a list is that another customer reading an idea may contribute to its development and elaboration. Also, a firm can monitor relevant newsgroups to discern what customers are saying about their products or services and those of competitors.

A firm can use the Web to pilot new ways of interacting with customers and other stakeholders. For example, it might experiment with different ways of marketing and delivering products and services. Or it can develop new communication channels with employees. Above all, firms need to be innovative in their use of the Web.

Inefficiency risk

Failing to match competitors' unit costs—**inefficiency risk**—is the third strategic challenge. A major potential use of the Internet is to lower costs by distributing as much information as possible electronically. For example, instead of mailing out glossy brochures, a firm can create a Web site containing all the details of the brochure and more. Of course, it must notify customers of the address of its Web site, and this can be done in corporate advertising. Consequently, some companies (e.g., Toshiba) now list both a toll-free number and Web address in their advertisements.

The cost of handling orders can also be reduced by using interactive forms to capture customer and order information. Web ordering, compared to processing an order via a toll-free number, is estimated to be about a third of the cost. This saving results from the customer's directly entering all data.

Also, because orders can be handled asynchronously, the firm can balance its work force because it no longer has to staff for peak ordering periods.

Consider the situation where a customer orders flowers via the Web (see Figure 6-1). In addition to entering delivery details, the customer can also specify special instructions and a message to appear on the card. Billing and credit card information (not shown in Figure 6-1) are also entered by the customer. Because the firm avoids this data entry, there are no misspellings of names or misunderstandings about delivery instructions or card message.

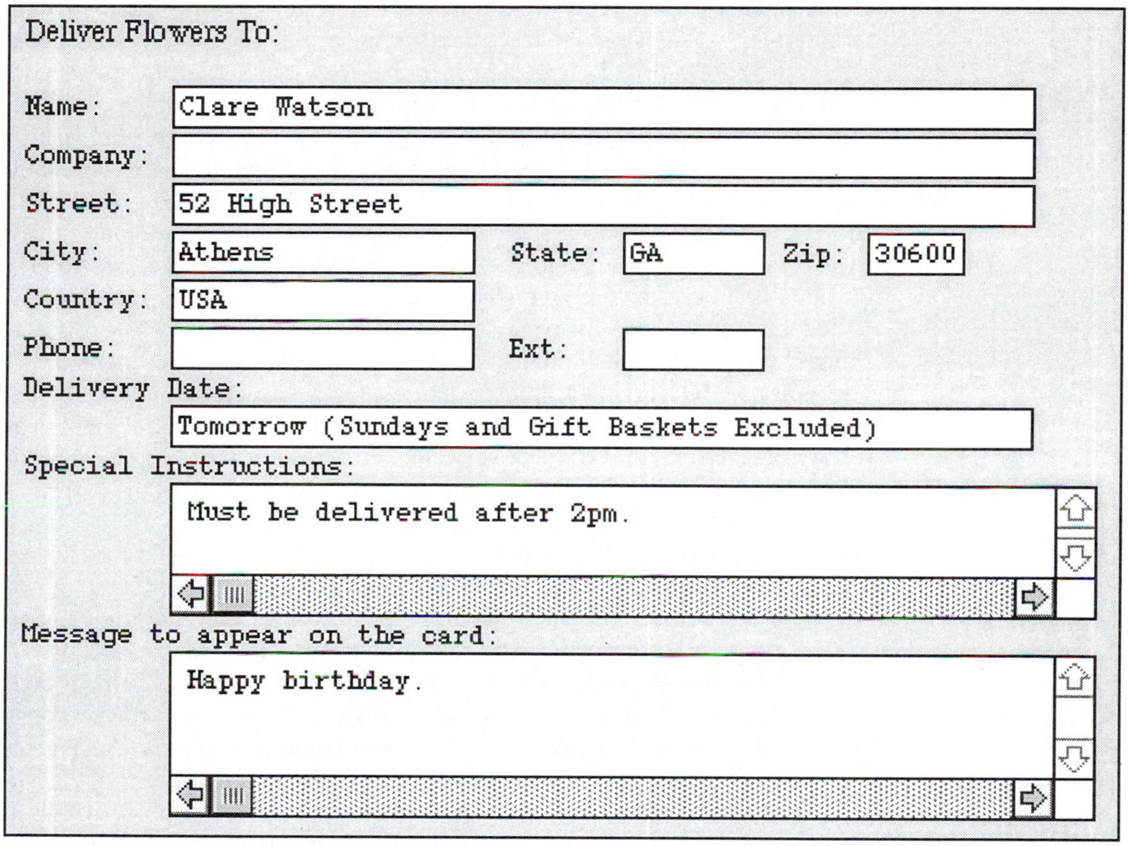
Deliver Flowers To:
Name: Clare Watson
Company:
Street: 52 High Street
City: Athens State: GA Zip: 30600
Country: USA
Phone: Ext:
Delivery Date:
Tomorrow (Sundays and Gift Baskets Excluded)
Special Instructions:
Must be delivered after 2pm.
Message to appear on the card:
Happy birthday.

Figure 6-1. Ordering using the Web

Your turn!

1. Visit General Motors and Carroll EMC (see footnotes 3 and 4 for the URLs). What similarities and differences do you note?
2. Find the Lands' End home page. Is it using the Web to reduce demand, innovation, or inefficiency risk?

Who should use the Web?

Each organization needs to consider whether it should have a Web presence, and if so, what should be the extent of its involvement. There are two key factors to be considered in answering these questions.

First, how many existing or potential customers are likely to be Web users? If a significant proportion of a firm's customers are Web users, then it should have a presence; otherwise it is missing an opportunity to inform customers of its products and services. The Web is user friendly and an extremely convenient source of information for many customers. If a firm does not have a home page, there is the risk that potential customers, attracted by the Web's ease of use, will flow to competitors who have a Web presence. Industrial marketers, companies who market to other businesses, are likely to find many of their customers already have access to the Web. Thus, it is not surprising to find that General Electric[7] has a significant Web presence. Another consumer segment with widespread access are advanced computer users, such as information systems specialists. Consequently, many of the hardware (e.g., DEC[8]) and software (e.g., Adobe[9]) firms have Web pages. Many college faculty, staff, and students have Web access, and most universities have home pages. Companies that recruit graduates, such as Andersen Consulting,[10] are likely to find that a Web presence is an effective communication medium.

Second, what is the **information intensity** of a company's products and services? An information-intense product is one that requires considerable information to describe it completely. For example, how do you describe a CD to a potential customer? Ideally, you would use text for the album notes and list the tunes, artists, and playing time; graphics to show the CD cover; sound for a sample of the music; and a video clip to show the artist performing. As you can see, a CD is information intensive because you need a great deal of information to describe it. Consequently, E. R. M. (Editions de la Rue Margot, Paris) has a Web catalogue of twentieth century music by present-day masters of new *classical* music. Visitors to its home page,[11] after viewing the CD cover and hearing portions of recordings, can order many of the featured CDs.

Many industrial products (e.g., computers and chemicals) are information intensive. Du Pont Lubricants,[12] with its extensive data on the properties of krytox fluorinated oils, provides an excellent example of how the Web can efficiently deliver very detailed product information to customers.

The two parameters, number of customers on the Web and product information intensity, can be combined to provide a simple model (see Figure 6-2) for determining which companies should be using the Web. Organizations falling in the top-right quadrant are prime candidates because many of their customers have Web access and their products have a high information content. Firms in the other quadrants, particularly the lower-right quadrant, have

---

7. http://www.ge.com:80/

8. http://www.digital.com/

9. http://www.adobe.com:80/

10. http://www.ac.com/recruit/map.htm

11. http://www.interaccess.com:80/users/numusic/

12. http://www.lubricants.dupont.com:80/

less need to establish a Web site, although any company with high information content products and services should be gearing up for a significant Web presence because many of its customers probably surf the Net.

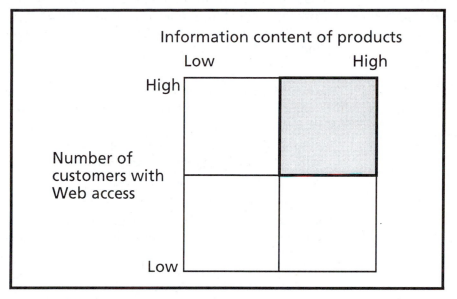

Figure 6-2. Web presence grid

Customers, of course, are not the only group with whom an organization may wish to communicate. Other stakeholders, those groups or individuals that can determine the future of an organization, can also be a communication target. Hence, some firms (e.g., MassMutual Consolidated[13])use the Web to provide financial reports to investors or attract new employees (e.g., Microsoft[14]). When many stakeholders have Web access, it becomes a general tool for communicating with them.

Your turn!

1. Visit DuPont Lubricant's page and note the level of detail provided.
2. How is Adobe using the Web to support customers?
3. Identify some organizations that are ideal candidates for the Web because their products have a high information content and many of their customers are likely to be Web users.

---

13. http://www.massmutual.com/finance.html
14. http://www.microsoft.com/pages/services/jobops/toplevel.htm

How can an organization use the Web?

Just suggesting that an organization should use the Web is often not very helpful. Managers frequently find it more useful to have models to focus their thinking and examples to stimulate creativity. In this section, two models are presented: the customer service life cycle and Integrated Internet Marketing. Each component of these models is accompanied by an illustrative case. The combination of a business model and an example should kindle generation of thoughts for Web use.

Customer service life cycle

The **customer service life cycle**[15] separates the service relationship with a customer into four major phases (see Figure 6-3), which are:

❖ **Requirements**: assisting the customer to determine needs (e.g., photographs of a product, video presentations, textual descriptions, articles or reviews, sound bytes of a CD, and downloadable demonstration files);

❖ **Acquisition**: helping the customer to acquire a product or service (e.g., on-line order entry, downloadable software);

❖ **Ownership**: supporting the customer on an ongoing basis (e.g., interactive on-line user groups, on-line technical support, frequently asked questions, resource libraries, newsletters, on-line renewal of subscriptions);

❖ **Retirement**: helping the client to dispose of the service or product (e.g., on-line resale, classified ads).

Examples for each major phase demonstrate how some organizations are currently using the Web.

Requirements. Hotel chain Promus[16] helps customers determine which of its three chains matches their travel plans. As an example, for its Embassy Suites, it shows a photo of a typical room and hotel. A complete directory of hotels with telephone numbers for reservations is provided for more than 30 countries. The information provided for each hotel includes: locale data; directions to the hotel; a description of the hotel and nearby attractions, restaurants, businesses, and cities; and a complete list of the hotel's facilities. Compared to a paper directory, the Web is far easier to use and contains considerably more detail.

Selecting a computer is a difficult task because there are many manufacturers offering a wide range of configurations. Dell Computer[17] provides complete details of each of its models, including specification of the hardware, pre-installed software, and available options (see Figure 6-4).

Once you have made your fortune on the Web, you may want to indulge in the ultimate in automotive conspicuous consumption—a Rolls-Royce. To help you decide your requirements—the Flying Spur, Corniche Convertible,

15. Ives, B.; Learmonth, G. P. The information systems as a competitive weapon. *Communications of the ACM*. 1984, 27 (12): 1193-1201.

16. http://www.promus.com/

17. http://www.us.dell.com/

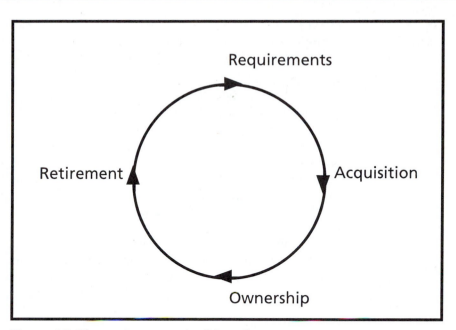

Figure 6-3. The customer service life cycle

Microprocessor

Microprocessor type	3.3-V P54C Pentium chip
Microprocessor speeds	75/50 MHz internal/external
	90/60 MHz internal/external
	100/66 Mhz internal/external
Internal cache	8 KB instruction
	8 KB data
Math coprocessor	internal
Microprocessor socket	ZIF

Figure 6-4. Detail for the Dell Dimension XPS

or Silver Spur III—check out Rolls-Royce of Beverly Hills.[18] Actually, this organization makes little use of the Web's capabilities because it simply displays a photo of the car. It would be interesting to see technical details, options, dashboard display, and maybe hear the sound of the Rolls-Royce cruising at 70 m.p.h. The list price would be quite useful, but then if you have to ask, you probably cannot afford a Rolls-Royce.

Using the Web for requirements information reduces the time and cost of delivering information to customers. Furthermore, a well-designed Web site can accelerate information retrieval by helping the customer navigate to needed information. Organizations can go even further; an expert system

---

18. http://www.clark.net/pub/networx/autopage/dealers/de001.html

could be used to ensure customers find the most relevant information. For example, Dell could use a series of questions (e.g., Will you use the system for desktop publishing?) to quickly narrow the range of feasible computers.

Acquisition. Many customers know how to buy flowers via the telephone—you simply dial 1-800-FLOWERS or the toll-free number of any florist. However, when you order by phone, you may find it hard to visualize the floral arrangement because you must rely on the order taker's verbal description. And remember the time the recipient's name was misunderstood—it certainly deflated the impact of the flowers. Web ordering solves both of these problems. You can see photos of the floral arrangements and enter the message to accompany the flowers. Once you provide credit card information, the order is complete. Many florists (e.g., Lane and Lenge[19]) now take orders over the Web.

Just about any item can be sold on the Web. For example, if you are concerned about the proportion of lead in the paint of an old house, you can order a $12.95 lead testing kit.[20] In addition to the order form, the page gives facts about lead and describes how to use the testing kit. The Web offers the opportunity for a small business, maybe with a single product, to reach an international market.

Hi-Studio Photo Art Gallery[21] features a Web display of the work of three photo artists. After viewing the photos, you can place an electronic order. You can also read about the photographers.

Web ordering has two major advantages. First, the customer enters the data into the computer, thus reducing the need for employees to do this task. Second, the firm has less need to synchronize its activities with its customers. For instance, a firm that receives many phone orders during the evening will have to employ sufficient staff during that period to handle peak traffic. As a result, if it is particularly concerned with customer service, it may well be over-staffed for much of the period because it is carrying slack to handle the peak load. While orders received via the Web should be handled expeditiously, the firm has better control over the scheduling of its employees because it breaks the nexus between the customer and the order taker.

Ownership. Every household in America is served by the U. S. Postal Service (USPS).[22] In terms of the customer service life cycle, each household owns a postal service that delivers mail to its address. USPS can make this service more efficient if every customer uses the full nine-digit ZIP code for addressing mail. Its Web site, as well as including details of current postal charges, has an interactive form that permits retrieval of the full ZIP for any U.S. address (see Figure 6-5). Simply complete the form, click on the Submit button (not shown in Figure 6-5), and within a few seconds the full ZIP is displayed. Imagine the cost savings if every consumer used this service.

---

19. http://plaza.xor.com/lane/start/lane.html
20. http://branch.com:80/epa/
21. http://www.cybermalls.com/cybernet/histudio/index.htm
22. http://www.usps.gov/

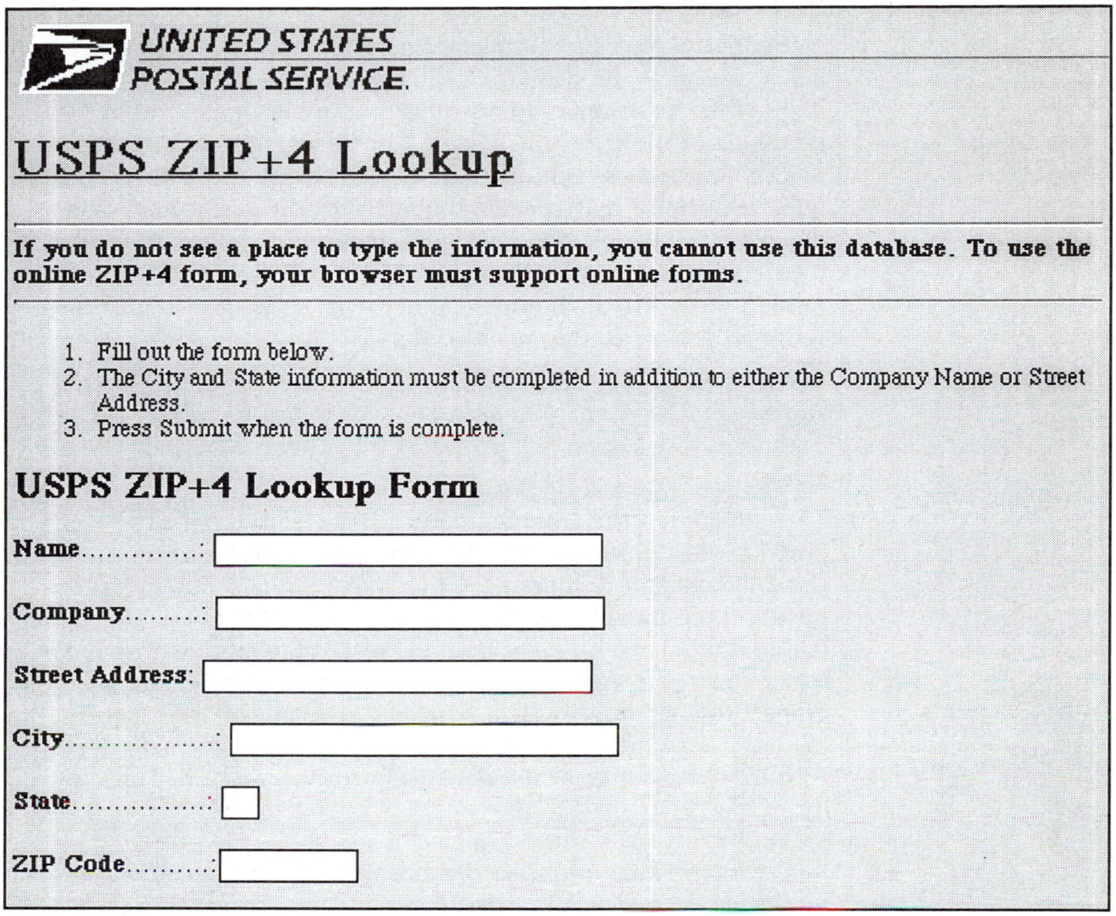

UNITED STATES POSTAL SERVICE.

USPS ZIP+4 Lookup

If you do not see a place to type the information, you cannot use this database. To use the online ZIP+4 form, your browser must support online forms.

1. Fill out the form below.
2. The City and State information must be completed in addition to either the Company Name or Street Address.
3. Press Submit when the form is complete.

USPS ZIP+4 Lookup Form

Name.............:

Company.........:

Street Address:

City.............:

State.............:

ZIP Code.........:

Figure 6-5. ZIP lookup

Checks are still widely used, even in an era of credit cards and electronic funds transfer, and account holders need periodically to order new checks. Citibank customers can now use the Web to select the design of their checks and place the order.[23] By using the Web, Citibank has found a convenient way to help its customers order new check books.

Federal Express (or FedEx) has built a business based on rapid delivery of letters and parcels. Many businesses and consumers use FedEx and similar services to ensure that items arrive on time. To reassure its customers, FedEx offers a tracking service. If you know the item's tracking code, you can find its current status by completing a form on the FedEx Web site.[24]

---

23. http://www.tti.com/

24. http://www.fedex.com

Safe as the mall

Network manager Ben Rothke claims shopping on the Internet is just as safe as shopping at the mall. He claims that the few hackers on the Internet scanning for credit card numbers are outnumbered by the many more devious people rummaging through trash bins at discount stores searching for discarded charge-card slips. A cash register operator may see more than 100 credit card numbers in a day. Very few people think twice about giving a restaurant worker their credit card in order to pay for their meal. People do not seem to be too concerned about revealing their credit card numbers—writing them on checks and fax orders.

Every major credit card company offers some protection for consumers. Purchasers can "charge back" or refuse to pay for certain purchases. Consumers are protected from misuse of their charge cards.

Thus, Rothke asserts that the Internet threat is minimal when compared to the current security breaches occurring hourly in many retail outlets and restaurants. Of course there is a threat, but we need to keep things in perspective. The Internet is not completely secure, but it is no different from the rest of the retail world. Electronic commerce poses no greater danger to consumers than many other forms of payment.

Adapted from: Rothke, B. Shopping the Internet is safe as buying at the mall. *PCWeek*. April 10, 1995: 55.

The three preceding examples demonstrate how organizations are using the Web during the ownership phase of the customer service life cycle. Notice that in each case, the organization is improving customer service and lowering its costs. The U.S. Postal Service will save on mail processing if more people use the full ZIP. Citibank can reduce the number of glossy brochures of check designs it mails to customers. It could even go one step further and interactively show customers how the check will look once their preferences are given. FedEx can reduce the number of service personnel required to answer phone queries about the status of a letter or parcel.

Retirement. Most of the organizations using the Web for the retirement phase of the customer service life cycle are in recycling. The Global Recycling Network (GRN)[25] is an electronic market to help businesses find possible trading partners for the sale of recyclable goods—raw materials, industrial by-products, used or rebuilt equipment, or unwanted machinery. Subscribers to GRN's on-line database add new trade opportunities every day. Businesses connected to GRN can make real-time buy and sell offers. Because GRN is on the Web, the service is international and can link companies anywhere.

---

25. http://grn.com/grn/

Power Express,[26] which sells batteries, provides details of how to recycle used batteries. Advice on how to recycle or re-use laser and ink-jet cartridges is supplied by Ribbon-Jet Trek.[27]

The Web seems to be particularly well-suited to support recycling because the market for used goods is rarely well-organized. The problem is that it is often difficult for buyers and sellers to find each other. Most markets for used products are local (e.g., the classified advertisements in the local newspaper). Going global with the Web greatly expands the size of the market and increases the potential of buyers and sellers finding each other. This is true for many markets that are difficult to sustain regionally.

Your turn!

1. Visit the Promus site and select a hotel for your next vacation.
2. Use the USPS Web page to determine the full ZIP of John Wiley & Sons' New York office.
3. Take each phase of the customer service life cycle (e.g., requirements) and find Web sites that illustrate support for this phase. Send your answer to Rick Watson (rwatson@uga.cc.uga.edu) so he can add this information to this book's Web site.[28] If selected, your contribution will be acknowledged, therefore you may wish to include the address of your home page so we can link to it.

Integrated Internet Marketing (I²M)

The interactive and multimedia capabilities of the Web, combined with other Internet facilities such as e-mail's support for personal and mass communication, present a range of tools for interacting with customers. Furthermore, the Web can provide easy-to-use, front-end to back-end applications using, for example, databases[29] and expert systems technology. Consequently, the Internet offers an excellent basis for a variety of marketing tactics, and we can develop a model for **Integrated Internet Marketing** (I²M).[30] [31]

---

26. http://www.baynet.com/powerexpress.html

27. http://usa.net/ca/casual.htm

28. http://www.negia.net/~webbook

29. For example, see the MIS faculty directory, which is stored on an SQL database and accessed via the Web (http://webfoot.csom.umn.edu/isworld/facdir/home.htm).

30. Portions of this section are adapted from Zinkhan, G. M.; Watson, R. T. Advertising trends: innovation and the process of creative destruction. *Journal of Business Research.* forthcoming.

31. Some of these ideas are based on Schultz, D. E.; Tannenbaum, S. I.; Lauterborn, R. F. *The new marketing paradigm: integrated marketing communications.* Lincolnwood, IL: NTC Business Books, 1994.

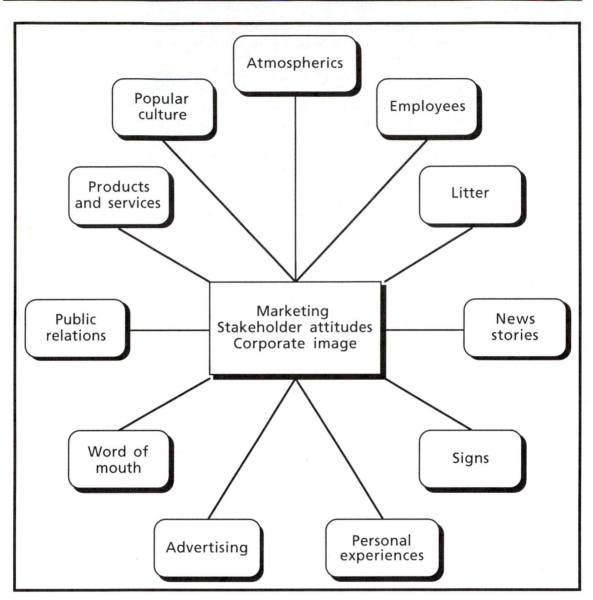

Figure 6-6. Components and processes that influence corporate image and customer attitudes

I²M (see Figure 6-6) is the coordination of Internet facilities to market products and services, shape stakeholders' (customers in particular) attitudes, and establish or maintain a corporate image. The central idea of I²M is that an organization should coordinate its use of the Internet to develop a coherent, synchronous marketing strategy. The following examples demonstrate how some organizations use particular features of the Web for elements of the I²M model, and the section concludes with an example of one organization's coordinated use of the Internet to market its products and services.

Atmospherics. Many organizations are interested in the ambiance or *atmospherics* their establishment creates for the customer. The Web provides an opportunity for customers to experience an organization's atmospherics without actually being there. For example, Alberto's nightclub (introduced in Chapter 1) in Mountain View, California[32] stimulates interest by creating an aura of excitement and action. The visual on its home page exudes the ethos of the club (Figure 6-7). An accompanying photo of the nightclub shows a crowded dance floor of young people.

Figure 6-7. Alberto's nightclub

If customers are reluctant to visit Alberto's because they can't dance the salsa, then they can step into the virtual ballroom where the dance step is displayed. Voice instructions, male or female steps, are available to help with the timing of the dance's steps. Instructions are available for eleven other dances. If personal lessons are desired, the customer can see a photo of the attractive instructors. Alberto's also provides a map for finding the nightclub.

Alberto's can go further by adding a video clip of the dance floor crowd and including some dance music. These additions would enhance the on-line atmosphere of a night at Alberto's.

Employees. E-mail and lists have become effective methods of communicating with employees, particularly for highly dispersed international organizations. Problems can be swiftly pushed up the hierarchy and decisions distributed quickly throughout the organization. As a result, a marketing problem in Hong Kong can be solved by an executive in Germany, and within minutes, the solution can be distributed to all relevant employees. Effective

32. http://albertos.com/albertos/

use of electronic communication permits rapid problem detection. Because policy changes can be distributed inexpensively and instantly, the organization can gain a high degree of consistency in its communications with employees and other stakeholders.

Also, an organization can develop a Web application focusing on employee communication. Instead of an in-house newsletter, the Web can be used to keep employees informed of company developments. The advantage is that previous issues of the newsletter can be made available, perhaps on a WAIS server, and there can be links to other related articles. For example, a story on new health benefits can have links to the firm's benefits policy manual.

Use of e-mail and the Web should lead to consistent internal communication, a necessary prerequisite of consistent external communication with customers, suppliers, shareholders, and other parties. A well-informed employee is likely to feel greater involvement with the organization and more able to perform effectively.

Litter. The discarded Big Mac wrapper blowing across the highway does little for MacDonald's corporate image. On the Internet, an advertisement arriving along with other e-mail may be perceived by some readers as highly offensive electronic pollution. An Arizona lawyer who posted an advertisement to millions of Internet users aroused considerable ire. The avalanche of e-mail complaints to him crashed his Internet service supplier's computer 15 times. The reaction spawned a program, based in Finland, that seeks out mass postings and deletes them. Of course, this raises the issue of who has the right to decide what advertising, or any other message for that matter, should be censored. Also, do some countries become havens for electronic terrorists whose programs wander the Internet, destroying what they consider improper or inappropriate?

News stories. Traditionally, organizations have relied on news media and advertisements to transmit their stories to the customer. Naturally, the use of intermediaries can pose problems. For example, news stories, not reported as envisaged, can result in the customer receiving a distorted, unintended message. When dealing with the Pentium hullabaloo, Intel's CEO Groves used the Internet to communicate directly with customers.

Signs. Most organizations prominently display their logos and other identifying signs on their buildings, packaging, and other visual points of customer contact. There has been a clear transfer of this concept to the Web. A corporate logo frequently is visually reinforced by placing it on each Web page.

Organizations can be extremely creative in their use of signs. Reykjavik Advertising,[33] with a collection of pages for a variety of Icelandic clients, makes clever use of the puffin, Iceland's national bird. Reykjavik Advertising's so-called traffic puffin indicates movement relative to a page hierarchy—back, up or forward, respectively (see Figure 6-10). It is an interesting

---

33. http://arctic.msg.net/MainSquare/MS.html

alternative to the bland arrows of a Web browser. The traffic puffin appears on each page. After viewing the pages, a clear impression of the resourceful use of the puffin remains. A new medium creates opportunities for reinventing signs.

Figure 6-8. Innovative use of a sign

Personal experience. Customers often prefer to try products before buying, and some software providers take advantage of this preference. Qualcomm[34] widely distributes a freeware version of Eudora, an e-mail package. Customers who adopt the freeware version can easily upgrade to a commercial version, available for around $40, which offers some appealing additional features. In Qualcomm's case, the incentive to upgrade is increased functionality. Another approach is taken by game maker Storm Impact, which distributes TaskMaker[35] as freeware. The full functionality of the game is available to play the first two tasks; however, the next eight tasks require payment of $25. On receipt of payment, a registration code to unlock the remaining tasks is e-mailed so that the next task can be tackled immediately.

Advertising. The hyperlink, a key feature of the Web, permits a reader to jump to another Web site by clicking on a link. An advertiser can place hyperlink signs or logos at relevant points on the Web so that interested readers may be enticed to link to the advertiser's Web site. For example, Prentice-Hall pays ISWorld Net[36] to display its logo prominently on ISWorld Net's home page, which provides an entry point to Web resources for IS academics and professionals. As a publisher of information systems textbooks, Prentice-Hall anticipates that potential adopters will follow the link to the Web site, where they can find details of relevant books, including sample chapters and support materials.

Hyperlinks are the billboards of the information highway. They are most valuable when they appear on Web pages read by potential consumers. As it is very easy to record the number of links from one page to another, it will be simple for advertisers to place a value on a particular hyperlink and for the owners of these pages to demand an appropriate rent.

34. http://www.qualcomm.com/

35. ftp:wuarchive.wustl.edu:system/mac/info-mac/game/task-maker-20.hqx

36. http://www.isworld.org/isworld.html

Measuring the effectiveness of Web advertising

Advertisers have always been concerned with measuring the effectiveness of their messages. Some typical questions for which they would like to find answers are: How many people saw the message? Did they spend time reading the message or just flip by it?

Open Markets, Inc. of Cambridge, MA has recently introduced WebReporter, software to analyze a Web site's traffic. Most Web servers log every access and record the address of the client requesting information and the date and time of the request. WebReporter analyzes a log file to create customized reports containing information such as the user's geographic area (e.g., country) and domain (commercial, government, or education), which pages were accessed, and the start and end times of each request. It can also be used to determine whether a site is being accessed by customers or competitors.

WebReporter offers firms the opportunity to experiment with different page designs and measure their impact. For example, a firm could have three designs for the same content page (e.g., information on a particular product) and by varying which page is displayed, it can gather data on which of the three alternatives is viewed longest (the difference between the start and end time of the request).

Adapted from: Anthes, G. H. Here come more Web tools: products emerge to manage and analyze site traffic. *Computerworld*. August 7, 1995: 55.

Word of mouth. Gossip and idle chatter around the water fountain are now complemented by lists and usenet. The impact of these electronic media can be quite profound as Intel discovered when the flaw in the Pentium chip was revealed in a message on the Internet. The incident was quickly conveyed to millions of Pentium customers, who bombarded Intel with e-mail. Indeed, Intel's CEO fueled discontent by posting an Internet message downplaying the problem and defending the company's decision to continue to produce defective chips. His Internet naivete (he used another executive's e-mail account to release the statement) was viewed negatively by the Internet community.

Word of mouth does not adequately describe the situation when a single electronic message can reach hundreds of thousands of people in a matter of minutes. It's more like a tsunami gathering momentum and crashing on the corporate doorstep before managers realize even a ripple of discontent. Bad news travels extremely fast on the Internet. Corporations are now monitoring lists and usenet groups that discuss their products and those of their competitors. As a result, they can quickly detect emerging problems and respond to statements that may be incorrect. Eavesdropping on customers' conversations is an important source of market intelligence, and it is becoming an important element of public relations.

Public relations. When IBM[37] announced its takeover bid for Lotus,[38] it used the Internet to reach its stakeholders, media, and Lotus employees. Once the financial markets had been notified, IBM's Web page featured the letter from IBM CEO Louis Gerstner to Jim Manzi, Lotus CEO. Also included were the internal memo to IBM employees, press release, audio clip of Gerstner explaining the offer, and a transcript of Gerstner's 45-minute news conference. By the end of the day, 23,000 people had accessed the Web page—about double the normal traffic. In contrast, Lotus' page had a four-paragraph statement from Manzi, but a company spokesperson said Lotus would respond when it had more to say about the offer.[39]

As IBM demonstrated, the Web can be an effective public relations tool. The advantage is that a company can immediately transmit its message to stakeholders without relying on intermediaries, such as newspapers and TV, to redistribute messages. Of course, mass mailing is also a method for directly reaching stakeholders, but a letter lacks the recency and multimedia features of the Web. Now that IBM has led the way, expect to see greater use of the Web for public relations.

Products and services. The Web has become a popular medium for the distribution of product information. When Dell[40] announced a new range of notebook computers, its Web server received 16,000 hits in one day. Compaq[41] has installed a server to provide customers with technical support, free software patches, and upgrades. Offering product support through the Web provides several advantages. First, it's a twenty-four hour, global service. Regardless of geographic location, all customers with Web access can use the service. Second, it's low cost. Customers help themselves to the information they want. Third, customers can tailor their search to meet their needs, providing the supplier has a rich, structured Web site. Fourth, information can be easily updated as required. There are no out-of-date brochures.

Computer firms struggle to solve hardware and software problems for a multitude of customers. This is a problem that can easily spiral out of control. One approach is to let customers solve each other's problems. As sure as there is one customer with a problem, there is another who has solved it or who would love the opportunity to tackle a puzzler. If customers can be convinced to solve each other's problems, then this creates the possibility of lowering the cost of customer service and raising customer satisfaction levels.

Thus, the real task is to ensure that the customer with the problem finds the customer with the solution. Apple has developed a simple system for improving customer service by creating virtual groups who support each other, reducing the number of people that Apple has to support.

---

37. http://www.ibm.com/

38. http://www.lotus.com/

39. Adapted from: Associated Press. Internet industries: latest merger info on IBM-Lotus? Check cyberspace. *Athens Banner-Herald*. Athens, GA; June 8, 1995; A: 12.

40. http://www.dell.com/

41. http://www.compaq.com/

In December 1994, Apple established two electronic lists, one devoted to Macintosh Internet client software and the other dedicated to discussing Macintosh Internet server software. Apple set up the lists and announced their creation in a weekly electronic newsletter that reaches 140,00 Macintosh users. The lists have roughly 1500 and 1000 subscribers, respectively, and each averages 14 messages per day. Typically, a problem will receive several responses within a few hours. For example, the concise, smug answer to the problem posed in Figure 6-11 was posted two hours after the question appeared.

At 21:08 3/28/95, ... wrote:

>I would like to put our network on the internet before we get the ISDN or 56k

>line installed. Is it possible to use a 288 modem and put our small lan on the

>net. I know I can put one computer on use Config PPP but I want to put a few

>Macs on and keep the dial up connection up continuously.

>

ISP's modem ---[phone line]--- Modem ------ router ---[ethernet]--- LAN

Easy.

Table 6-2: A list interaction

Quite encouraged by this venture, Apple now supports four lists, and the concept is being extended.

Popular culture. If you have seen *Forrest Gump,* you may remember the scene in which Forrest is riding his lawn mower. The maker's name is quite prominent for a few seconds. Firms have discovered that popular culture—movies, songs, and live performances—can be used to publicize their goods. As the Internet develops, we may see clearly labeled products appear in virtual network games. Indeed, a popular MUD, Genocide, already features well-known fast food stores.[42]

TidBITS - a case study of I²M

TidBITS,[43] an electronic newsletter for Macintosh aficionados, started by Adam. C. Engst in April 1990, illustrates how Internet resources can help a company develop an integrated marketing strategy (see Table 6-2). E-mail is used to collect editorial material from software and hardware suppliers as well as writers. Engst needs to market his newsletter to major Macintosh suppliers because they provide material for stories. For example, Apple supplies details of how to obtain the release of a software upgrade. Subscribers can send questions or comments to the publisher.[44] The e-mail addresses of the

---

42. As noted by Ned Watson, a teenage Internet addict.

43. http://www.dartmouth.edu/pages/TidBITS/TidBITS.html

44. For example, a response for information for this chapter was received within one day.

newsletter's sponsors are given. Readers can easily contact sponsors by cutting and pasting the e-mail address from the newsletter into the "to:" field of an e-mail program and composing a message. In addition to receiving revenue from sponsors, Engst writes books on the Internet. These are mentioned at the end of each newsletter and when a new book is released, he tells how to e-mail the publisher to order a copy.

The estimated 140,000 *TidBITS* readers in over 40 countries receive their copies electronically. A list is a simple, elegant system for handling distribution. The entire process is automated. Consumers send a message to subscribe to or drop from the list. All the publisher has to do is send the newsletter to the list, and the server takes care of the rest.

Engst's Internet books are packaged with a diskette containing useful software (e.g., e-mail and FTP programs). However, there is a limit to how much software you can place on a diskette, and new releases appear frequently. By operating an FTP server, Engst provides his customers with access to an extensive collection of the latest freeware and shareware. The FTP program packaged with the book provides all readers with ready access to the FTP server.

An electronic repository of past issues is stored on the Web, and this can be searched electronically via WAIS. Thus, subscribers needn't worry about keeping past copies of the newsletter as all issues are conveniently available. In addition, links to sponsors' home pages are displayed.

Engst's understanding of the Internet enables him to market his products effectively, maintain contacts with his suppliers, and connect his sponsors to customers. He provides his customers with a wide range of services that require a minimum of administration.

Table 6-3: The integrated marketing of *TidBITS*

Service	Use
Electronic mail	Communication with sources of editorial material
	Personal responses to subscribers
	Subscribers' contact with sponsors
	Orders for books
List server	Distribution of the newsletter
FTP	Access to software accompanying books and mentioned in the newsletter
World Wide Web	Full text of past issues of TidBITS
	Access to sponsors
WAIS	Searches through past issues of TidBITS

Conclusion

The Internet, and the Web in particular, offers many opportunities for organizations to redesign their present business practices to reduce demand, innovation, and inefficiency risk. By using frameworks and examples of other companies' applications, businesses can set out to identify their opportunities. Of course, a good dose of Web surfing, just browsing around to get a feel for what's happening, might also lead to those serendipitous discoveries that provide elucidating glimpses into how an organization can exploit the Internet. Whatever approach you take, you must recognize that the Internet cannot be ignored.

Key terms and concepts

acquisition
customer convergence
customer service life cycle
demand risk
inefficiency risk
information intensity
innovation risk

Integrated Internet Marketing (I²M)
market segmentation
mass marketing
one-to-one marketing
ownership
requirements
retirement

- -

Exercises

1. Choose three businesses with which you are familiar. Of the three strategic challenges, which do you think is the most threatening to each of these businesses? How might they use the Web to reduce the risks?

2. Describe the approach you would use to increase the flow of innovative ideas from customers.

3. Identify some information-intensive products. How could the Web be used to promote them?

4. Identify some information-intensive services. How could the Web be used to promote these services?

5. Check out the *What's New?* link that you will find on many home pages and report any innovative uses of the Web. Do they fit the customer service life cycle or I²M model? If not, e-mail us so we can share your finding with other readers via this book's Web home page.

6. Meet with a business and, using the models in this chapter, help it brainstorm how it might use the Web.

- -

A Special Characters

"	&quote;	Ê	&Ecirc;	Ò	&Ograve;
&	&amp;	ê	&ecirc;	ò	&ograve;
<	&lt;	È	&Egrave;	Ø	&Oslash;
>	&gt;	è	&egrave;	ø	&oslash;
Á	&Aacute;	Ë	&Euml;	Õ	&Otilde;
á	&aacute;	ë	&euml;	õ	&otilde;
Â	&Acirc;	fi	&THORN;	Ö	&Ouml;
â	&acirc;	fl	&thorn;	ö	&ouml;
À	&Agrave;	Í	&Iacute;	ß	&szlig;
à	&agrave;	í	&iacute;	Ú	&Uacute;
Å	&Aring;	Î	&Icirc;	ú	&uacute;
å	&aring;	î	&icirc;	Û	&Ucirc;
Ã	&Atilde;	Ì	&Igrave;	û	&ucirc;
ã	&atilde;	ì	&igrave;	Ù	&Ugrave;
Ä	&Auml;	Ï	&Iuml;	ù	&ugrave;
ä	&auml;	ï	&iuml;	Ü	&Uuml;
Æ	&AElig;	Ñ	&Ntilde;	ü	&uuml;
æ	&aelig;	ñ	&ntilde;	ÿ	&yuml;
Ç	&Ccedil;	Ó	&Oacute;	›	&eth;
ç	&ccedil;	ó	&oacute;	‡	&yacute;
É	&Eacute;	Ô	&Ocirc;		
é	&eacute;	ô	&ocirc;		

Glossary

Absolute addressing. A type of anchor address that indicates an object on a different server from the current Web page. The full URL must be specified in the anchor.

Acquisition. The second stage of the customer service life cycle during which the supplier helps the customer acquire a product or service.

Anchor. A type of HTML tag that indicates the name of the object to be retrieved by the browser from a server.

Backbone. In a computer network, the primary high-speed communications link between major computer centers to which other networks are connected.

Bandwidth. The term used as a measure of the capacity of a communication channel, expressed in bits per second.

Browser. Client software used on the Web to fetch and read documents on screen and print them, jump to other documents via hypertext, view images, and listen to audio files.

Centralized computer network. One in which there is one computer or a group of computers to which all other computers must be linked.

Clickable map. A graphical image on which sections act as hypertext links to other Web pages.

Client/server computing. A combination of clients and servers that provides the framework for distributing files across a network.

Client. A personal computer running an application that can access and display information on a server.

Codification. An organized method for storing data in a computer system.

Computer Network. An interconnected system of computers.

Computer. An electronic, automatic machine that manipulates and stores symbols based on instructions from the user.

Content area. The part of the Netscape window in which the actual HTML-formatted text and inline images of the current page are displayed.

Customer convergence. The Web marketing concept that firms must describe their products and services so that potential customers converge on the relevant Web pages.

Customer service life cycle. A model that delineates the service relationship with a customer into four phases: requirements, acquisition, ownership, and retirement.

Decentralized computer network. One in which there is no single computer or group of computers to which every other computer is linked.

Decryption. Conversion of encrypted text represented by characters into a readable form.

Default HTML file. The Web page file that is accessed automatically at a Web site when no HTML file is shown as a part of the URL.

Demand risk. The risk that changing demand or the collapse of markets significantly reduces demand for a firm's products or services.

Directory buttons. On the Netscape screen, a series of clickable buttons shown directly beneath the location window; they correspond to a special set of Web pages which the developers of Netscape believe to be useful to users.

Discussion list. A group of e-mail users who have all subscribed to a listserver to share their ideas on a particular topic.

Disk cache. In Netscape, the storage on disk of a number of recently visited Web pages.

Distribution. A measure of how widely information is shared.

Download. The process of shifting software or data from a central computer to a personal computer and saving it on disk.

Electronic document. An electronic form of a printed document.

Electronic mail (e-mail). An electronic technology that handles the sending and receiving of messages.

Encryption. The conversion of readable text into characters that disguise the original meaning of the text.

File transfer protocol (FTP). A protocol that supports file transfers over the Internet.

File protocol. The Web protocol used to access a local file.

Forms. Areas in Web pages that can be filled in by the user and returned to the Web server for processing.

Gopher. A distributed document search and retrieval system.

Graphic elements. The term encompassing several elements, including color, motion, and resolution, that together result in the ability of a computer to show line drawings, pictures, or animation on a display screen.

Graphical user interface (GUI). An interface that uses pictures and graphic symbols to represent commands, choices, or actions.

Helper software. Software packages linked to the browser in such a way that they are invoked automatically when the user requests that an audio or video file be played or a large image is displayed.

Home page. The first page encountered at a Web site.

Hypertext Markup Language (HTML). A markup language used to create Web pages consisting of text, hypertext links, and multimedia elements.

HTML editor. An editor that enables the user to easily insert HTML tags and hypertext links to other files.

Hypertext Transfer Protocol (http). The protocol for moving hypertext files across the Internet.

Hypermedia. An extension of hypertext that includes graphics, video, sound, and music.

Hypertext. A method of linking related information in which there is no hierarchy or menu system.

Hypertext links. Links to other Web pages or Internet resources.

Inefficiency risk. The risk that a firm loses market share because it fails to match competitors' unit costs.

Information intensity. The degree of information required to describe completely a product or service.

Innovation risk. The risk that a firm fails to continually improve its products and services and loses market share to more innovative competitors.

Integrated Internet marketing (I²M). The coordination of Internet facilities to market products and services, shape stakeholder attitudes, and establish or maintain a corporate image.

Internet. A worldwide network of computers and computer networks in private organizations, government institutions, and universities, over which people share files, send electronic messages, and have access to vast quantities of information.

Internet operations. A variety of operations that can be carried out on the Internet including FTP, e-mail, Telnet, Gopher, and the World Wide Web.

Internet providers. Companies who specialize in linking organizations and individuals to the Internet as well as providing services to them.

List. A type of HTML tag that creates three types of lists: regular, menu, and descriptive.

Listserver. A program providing a set of e-mail functions that enables users to participate in electronic discussions.

Local files. Web files that are available from a local hard disk or network file server.

Location window. A text window located immediately beneath the toolbar in which the URL of the current page is displayed. It also can be used to enter a new URL.

Logical style. HTML syntax for specifying how a text string will be displayed by a browser. Each command corresponds to a logical representation of text (e.g., emphasis) that may be changed by the user of the browser (e.g., display *emphasis* as *bold*).

Map. See **clickable map.**

Market segmentation. The division of a market into segments based on demographic or other relevant variables in order to deliver more precisely an appropriate message to potential customers.

Markup language. A publishing industry term for describing the size, style, and position of each typographical element on a page.

Mass marketing. Broadcasting the same message to all potential customers.

Memory cache. In Netscape, the storage of recent Web pages in computer memory.

Menu bar. A menu bar at the top of the Netscape screen that provides users with a variety of options from which to choose.

Modem. A communications device that modulates computer signals into outgoing audio signals and demodulates incoming audio signals into computer signals.

Multimedia. A interactive combination of text, graphics, animation, images, audio, and video displayed by and under the control of a personal computer.

Multimedia files. Digitized images, videos, and sound that can be retrieved and converted into an appropriate human recognizable information by a client.

Multi user dimension or dungeon (MUD). A multiple-user, electronic game that is an ongoing drama with an electronically assembled cast exploring and interacting in cyberspace.

Newsgroups. See **USENet News.**

One-to-one marketing. Delivering a specific message to a particular customer, often assisted by a marketing database.

Opening home page. The Web page that is automatically loaded when Netscape is first accessed or the Home Toolbar button is clicked.

Ownership. The third stage of the customer service life cycle during which the supplier helps the customer maintain a product or service.

Page. An electronic document on the Web that contains text and hypertext links to multimedia elements and other pages that are stored on server computers.

Path. A portion of the URL which includes the name of the home page file plus any directories or folders in which it is located.

Portable Document Format (PDF). A form of electronic document created with Adobe's Acrobat Exchange that can be easily shared with anyone who has an Acrobat reader.

Phonebook. An electronic list of e-mail addresses of all persons at a particular location.

Physical style. A HTML syntax for specifying how a text string will be displayed by a browser. Each command corresponds to a physical representation of text (e.g., bold) that cannot be changed by the user of the browser.

Point and click operations. Operations that can be carried out simply by pointing at menu selections or icons representing operations and clicking the mouse button.

Point and click navigation. A method that involves using a mouse or other pointing device to position the pointer over a hypertext link or the menu bar, tool bar, location window, or directory buttons and clicking a button to retrieve a Web page or execute a corresponding command.

Port number. An internal address within a Web server.

Private key. A encryption key that is known only by the person sending and receiving encrypted messages.

Progress bar. An area at the bottom of the Netscape screen which uses both text and graphics to display the status of loading a Web page as well as to display other useful information.

Protocol. A formal set of rules for specifying the format and relationships when exchanging information between communicating devices.

Public key. A encryption key that is known to all persons who share encrypted communication with a particular person (who holds a private key).

Relative addressing. A type of anchor address that indicates an object on the same server as the Web page. Only the path portion of the URL is specified in the anchor.

Requirements. The first stage of the customer service life cycle during which the supplier helps the customer determine the attributes of the required product or service.

Retirement. The fourth and final stage of the customer service life cycle during which the supplier helps the customer dispose of a product or service.

Scroll bars. Horizontal and vertical bars in a browser that allow movement to parts of the Web page that are not currently on the screen.

Search engines. Software that has been developed to enable Web users to search for Web pages that contain desired topics.

Secure server. A Web server that provide users protection from having their messages read while being transmitted over the Internet.

Security area. An area of the Netscape screen which displays a door key; if the door key is displayed on a blue background, then the home page is considered secure.

Server address. The address of the computer on which the Web resource is stored.

Server. A computer on the Web running an application that manages a data store containing files of text, images, video clips, and sound.

Service resource. Another name for a protocol on the Web.

Shortcut keys. Key combinations that can be used instead of the mouse button; often uses the Ctrl key in conjunction with a letter.

Signing. An encryption method that ensures that a message is from a particular person.

Special characters. Non-ASCII characters that are created by HTML in the form &charactername; where & indicates the beginning of the character and ; indicates the end.

Status indicator. An area of the Netscape screen in which the Netscape corporate logo is displayed; it is animated in some way while a Web page is being loaded.

Table. A type of HTML tag that supports the presentation of a table containing a caption, column, row headers, and cell elements.

Tag. The basic component of HTML which describes to the Web browser how to display information.

TCP/IP (Transmission Control Protocol/Internet Protocol). The communication protocol of the Internet.

Telnet. The main Internet protocol for connecting to a remote machine.

Text (ASCII) file. A file in the form of readable text, as opposed to binary.

Title bar. The area at the top of the Netscape screen that displays the title of the current Web page.

Toolbar. A button bar located beneath the menu bar which consists of nine command buttons that provide quick access to important Netscape operations.

URL (Uniform Resource Locator). A standard means of consistently locating Web pages or other resources no matter where they are stored on the Internet.

USENET News (News). A vast set of discussion lists which can be accessed through the Internet.

Wide Area Information Services (WAIS). A project originally sponsored by a group of companies that is now owned by America Online. WAIS supports access to a wide variety of electronically published material.

Web directory. A hierarchically structured list of Web pages. Available from Netscape by clicking on the Net Directory button.

Web searching. The process of searching for Web pages of interest using a piece of software called a search engine.

Web page. A special type of document that contains hypertext links to other documents or to various multimedia elements.

Web sites. Internet server computers on which Web pages are stored.

Web page address. The Internet address at which a Web page is found.

World Wide Web (WWW). A body of software, a set of protocols, and conventions based on hypertext and multimedia techniques that make the Internet easy for anyone to browse and add contributions.

Index

handler application, 95
FrameMaker, 119
Frequently Asked Questions
    (FAQs), 103, 110
    for the Simpsons, 110
    for Seinfeld, 110

G

Gallup survey, 58
Georgia, University of, 106
General Electric, 130
General Motors, 126
Global Recycling Network (GRN),
    136
Goldman Sachs & Co., 10
Gopher, 7, 14, 24, 101, 113-114
    as Internet operation, 7, 24
    HTML for, 114
graphical user interface (GUI), 12,
    26, 30
graphics, 12, 23, 26, 28
    elements, 28
groupware, 16

H

Haagen-Dazs, 2
helper software, 36, 53
Heraclitus, 1
Hi-Studio Photo Art Gallery, 134
Hotel Chain Promus, 132
HyperCard, 9
hyperlinks, 23, 28-30, 37, 54-55, 76,
    85, 141
hypermedia, 23, 85
hypertext, 8-9, 12, 22-23, 29-30, 37,
    54-55, 57, 76, 113
    clickable links, 27, 29-30, 54-55
    definition of, 8
    example of, 9
    links, 9, 12-14, 23, 26-30, 37, 54-55
    proposal of, 9
    transfer protocol (http), 32, 34, 50,
        57
    use in Hypercard, 10
    use in Microsoft Windows, 10
Hypertext Markup Language
    (HTML), 27, 34, 75-94
    anchors, 85-90
    codes, 34, 68, 75-94
    formatted text, 53
    forms, 95
    heading levels, 78

lists, 83-84
loading an image, 80-91
logical styles, 80-81
maps, 95-96
physical styles, 80-81
purpose, 76
special characters, 96
tables, 93-94
tags, 39, 75-94
hypertext transfer protocol (http://
    ), 32, 34, 50, 57
    retrieving Web page with, 57

I

IBM, 3, 143
    compatible PCs, 29, 34
    Gerstner, Louis (CEO), 143
Iceland Air, 32
icons, 27-28
Illinois, University of, 26
images, 10-12, 23, 33
    GIF, 33, 80
    JPEG, 80
inefficiency risk, 128-129
information age, 21
information superhighway, 2
InfoSeek search engine, 72, 100-101
innovation risk, 128
Intel, 140
Intellimedia Sports, Inc., 17-18, 22,
    27, 30-32, 39-40, 45, 51, 59, 65
    address for, 30-32, 51
    in text form, 39
    printed page, 40
    Web page for, 18, 22, 28, 30, 35, 39-
        40, 51, 59, 65
Integrated Internet Marketing, 137-
    145
    advertising, 141
    atmospherics, 139
    employees, 139-140
    litter, 140
    news stories, 140
    personal experience, 141
    popular culture, 143
    products and services, 143
    public relations, 143
    signs, 140-141
    word of mouth, 142
Internal Revenue Service, 118
Internet, 4-8, 10, 12, 16, 23-25, 27, 33-
    34, 37, 50, 59, 63

access to, 63
address, 37
and Web, 7, 27, 37, 59, 72
backbone for, 7-8, 23
bandwidth, 33-34
catalog company, 120
commercial use, 6, 23, 119, 120
connection to, 8, 59
global communication, 16
growth in, 10, 23-24
MBone as part of, 12
operations, 6-7, 24
problems with, 23-25
provider, 7
protocol for, 5
publishing, 10
resources, 104-115
shopping, 136
traffic, 23
Unix-based, 23-25
Web as interface to, 104-115
Web sites on, 50, 72, 99
Internet Network Information
    Center (InterNIC), 37
interstate highway system, 7-8
Israel Information Service, 114
ISWorld Net, 141

J

Jimmy Buffett's Margaritaville, 18,
    32, 41- 45
    address for, 32
    clickable map for, 42
    e-mail to, 42
    form for, 41
Jobs, Steve, 69
John Wiley & Co., 32

K

Kaplan Education Centers, 37

L

Lane and Lenge, 134
Local area network (LAN), 7-8, 16
Lotus Development Corp., 3, 143
    Manzi, Jim (CEO), 143
Lotus Notes, 16
Lycos, 102
Lynx, 23

M

MacDonald's, 140

Web pages on, 13-14, 22
shortcut keys, 60
signing, 122
SimpleText, 38
sniffer programs, 119
Smarr, Dr. Larry, 21
Smith-Corona, 2, 126
South Africa, 17
spreadsheets, 93
Storm Impact, 141

T

T1 lines, 33
tag, 11, 39, 75-94
   client interpretation of, 11
   HTML, 75-94
Telecom Australia, 32
Telnet, 7, 14, 112-113
   HTML for, 112
   protocol, 112
Texas Tech University, 105
text files, 10, 12, 23
TidBITS, 144-145
   Engst, Adam C., 144
toolbar buttons, 27, 51, 53, 56-60
Toshiba, 129
Transmission Control Protocol/
   Internet Protocol (TCP/IP), 5

U

unicasting, 12
Uniform Resource Locator (URL),
   30-32, 37-38, 49-51, 53- 55, 57,
   70, 85, 90-91, 107
   as address of Web page, 30, 49
   entering, 55, 57, 107
   for images, 90-91
   for local file, 33-34, 50-51, 57
   for remote Web site, 33-34, 50-51
   default HTML file, 32
   in HTML anchor, 85, 107
   in location window, 53-54
   in Open location dialog box, 57
   parts of, 30-32
   path, 32, 50
   port, 31
   protocols for, 30-31
   saving, 70
   server address, 31
   service resource, see protocols for
United States Congress, 6
United States Postal Service, 134

Unix, 23
   and Internet, 23-25
   commands, 23
   difficulty in using, 24
   example of, 25
   server, 105
   workstations, 26
   X-Windows workstation, 24, 30,
   51
USENET Newsgroups, 7, 14, 24,
   100, 106-108
   as Internet operation, 24
   commercial use, 128
   common categories. 106
   HTML for, 107
   newsreaders for, 106

V

video files, 5, 10-12, 14-15, 23, 25
Visa, 126
VisiCalc, 26

W

Wall Street Journal, 10, 127
Watson, Richard, 5
   ear operation for, 5
Web, 7-8, 10-13, 22-24, 26-42,
   advertising, 126
   as Internet operation, 7
   as client/server software, 10-11,
   22
   browsers, 12-13, 23, 24, 26-42
   business applications of, 14, 17-18
   commerce on 17-18, 22, 32-32, 38,
   41, 50, 72, 99-103, 115, 117, 119,
   125-145
   commercial examples, 17-18, 32
   development of, 8
   growth in, 10
   history of, 8
   home page, 27
   hypertext in, 8-9
   navigating, 12
   ordering, 119, 134
   page address, 27
   protocols, 31
   resources, see protocols.
   searching, 29, 38, 72, 99-103, 115
   servers, 11-14, 22, 50, 117
   server addresses, 11, 50
   sites, 27, 50, 72

support of wide distribution of
   multimedia, 17
   use of tags, 11, 39, 75-94
   who should use, 130-131
Web book home page, 51, 53, 65, 68
   URL for, 51, 53
Web pages, 13-14, 27, 29-42, 49-51,
   54, 57, 63
   entering URL for, 57
   remote, 33-34, 50-51, 57, 59
   local, 33-34, 50-51, 57, 59
   secure, 54
   steps in retrieving, 57
WebCrawler, 38, 72, 102
WebObjects, 69
WebReporter, 142
What You See Is What You Get
   (WYSIWYG), 39
White House, The, 5, 28, 36
   address for, 11
   Conference on Small Business, 58
   home page for, 28
   Socks, 28, 36
Wide Area Information Servers
   (WAIS), 114-115, 140, 145
   relevance feedback, 115
   server, 140
   WAISGATE, 114
wide area networks, 16
word processing software, 68, 119
WordPerfect for Windows, 119
World Factbook, 115
World Phone Books, 105
World Wide Web, See Web
World Wide Web Worm, 38
Wozniak, Steve, 69

X

X-Windows workstation, 24, 30

Y

Yahoo, 38, 72, 102

Z

Zima Beverage, 33
   Web site for, 33